OMG!
What's Been Done with Jesus?

Bringing Christ Back to the Forefront

Eleanor ("Ellie") Parks

The Amazon Endure typeface was designed by 2K/DENMARK in 2025.
Template id: ST-414D415A-25-A01
Printed in The United States.
ISBN: 979-8-218-87343-1

DEDICATION

My wonderful son, Bryant Michael Parks, was a delight and easy to raise. I didn't have a clue what to do, how to be when you were born, but God did. You were always more righteous than I. I learned from you and still do. I'm proud of you! Michael, "like God," is an appropriate middle name God gave us to give you. I love you and your beautiful family, my family—Kelly, Amiyah, Azariah, and baby Ayla!

My parents, Catherine Marie and Richard James Parks, showed me how to remember God, be loving, and an honest citizen. You knew me—the good, the bad, the ugly, the quirky — but loved me anyway. Those exceptional Christmases are etched in my mind! Thanks!

My living siblings—Judith, Ronald, and John, and the three deceased eldest—Christine, Richard, Jr., and Carolyn. There's a piece of each of you in me, and I'm glad. I am because of all your input, advice, help, fights, and love. I love yall! Thanks.

My nieces and nephews—Caprice, Willie IV, Kimberly, Christopher, and Catherine. You rock! Stay in the Way, regardless of what comes, what goes. Proud of you all and love you. Thanks for all the money loans, too! LOL. (Yup, nieces and nephews lend money.) Christopher, your book on *Race, Faith, and Politics: 7 Questions Every African American Christian Must Answer"* inspired me to write this book. Thanks. All your children, too — my second-generation nieces and nephews. Love yall!

Table of Contents

ACKNOWLEDGMENTS

My cousin, donetta t. porter 'bka' Bonnie, Illustrative Designer, who completed the book graphics. Thanks for your designer's eye, patience, quick work, and price (LOL). It was great and easy working with you. Forever grateful. Love you!

and

My mentor, who got me started in Christian writing and helped make this publication possible, Marlene Bagnull, Founder and Director of Write His Answer Ministries. Her books and conferences are invaluable. She always pushes Jesus Christ! God bless you and thank you. Love you!

Tell Me the Story of Jesus

Song by Frances J. Crosby, pub.1880

Tell me the story of Jesus,
write on my heart every word.
Tell me the story most precious,
sweetest that ever was heard.
Tell how the angels in chorus,
sang as they welcomed His birth,
"Glory to God in the highest!
Peace and good tidings to earth."

Refrain:

Tell me the story of Jesus,
write on my heart every word.
Tell me the story most precious,
sweetest that ever was heard.

Fasting alone in the desert,
tell of the days that are past.
How for our sins He was tempted,
yet was triumphant at last.
Tell of the years of His labor,
tell of the sorrow He bore.
He was despised and afflicted,
homeless, rejected and poor.

Tell of the cross where they nailed Him,
writhing in anguish and pain.
Tell of the grave where they laid Him,
tell how He liveth again.
Love in that story so tender,
clearer than ever I see.
Stay, let me weep while you whisper,
love paid the ransom for me.

INTRODUCTION

No one noticed. I received no compliments or few acknowledgments of God's work in my life. I don't recall any motivating well-wishes or someone giving me encouraging spiritual words such as, "I see God is working in your life, Ellie! You're doing well. Keep going." I didn't receive a pat on the back showing they noticed the same God in me that was in them. Perhaps these were just my own insecurities, as my attitude was poor on some days. My words were harsh, and my expression was too stern. Other flaws, too, possibly made me seem un-Christian

I realized people might have focused on their ideal of what a Christian looks like, instead of seeing Jesus' work in my heart. Surely, I did not fit their mold. Experience has taught me, however, that recognition from others doesn't determine the reality of God's work in us.

Because I didn't feel supported or recognized as a woman of faith, I now approach others in the Christian community differently. I realize that life in Christ begins within and expresses itself outwardly—it's a heart matter that humans rarely judge accurately. We struggle to recognize someone's relationship with God because our perspective is often worldly, not divine. As 2 Corinthians 5:16 (NIV) asserts, *so from now on we regard no one from a worldly point of view.* (Have you ever seen that verse?)

As followers of Christ, we must go deep inside ourselves and admit (or confess) how there are so many factors, other than God, that shape our concept of Him—how we think He relates to us and others, or how we are to relate to Him. After all, a relationship with God is what He intended for us when He created the first man and woman.

Don't fret if your thinking is faulty; becoming and remaining close to God is possible. I compare it to when a mother conceives a child. During pregnancy, neither knows much about the other until birth. However, the relationship begins with conception, and both mother and baby experience each other in the womb. The baby senses the mother through oxygen and nutrients received via the umbilical cord. As the child grows, the mother's belly expands. The child moves, kicks, or curls up comfortably. The mother might feel as if her womb is a gym with a baby doing somersaults—as I felt with my son. But it's only when the child is born and enters the physical world that the bond deepens. Through the five senses and time spent together, mother and baby truly get to know each other. Now they can see, feel, hear, touch, smell, and taste one another.

God intends our relationship to be like this, even though He already knows us. A baby can only grow in the world by first exiting the mother's womb and then connecting with her, other humans, and the material world. Such is what happens in a new birth relationship with God.

This book is for anyone, regardless of their background or beliefs, including people who are exploring, doubting, or have lost their faith. Those who acknowledge God as supreme, pray to Him, or attend places where He's known, but have never personally met Him. If you're a younger Gen Z Christian, you might be confused because your faith includes practices like meditation, astrology, and New Age spirituality. Gen Xers, you question things but may still have religious beliefs, even if you don't go to church often or follow traditional practices; digital communities interest you. Millennials, you are spiritual but not religious; possibly doubt, some church hurt, or cultural shifts have caused you to deconstruct the faith or completely abandon it. Baby Boomers, you are known as a religious group, but perhaps you can see and fix some errors you passed down to the younger generation. Finally, for those of you in the Silent Generation, you have some great stories; maybe you will realize we still need to hear from you. Regardless of your age or spiritual journey, this book has something for you.

In the book, I share some excerpts from my journey of coming to know God through Jesus Christ, to show how God is real, wants to be known, and how He transforms lives. My stories provide evidence that Jesus can bring genuine change.

What I Believe

I believe, am convinced, and stand on what God has said about Himself in the Bible. He is the creator of the world and humankind (Genesis 1). He has always existed and will forever exist (Revelations 1:8). He is the beginning of things (Alpha) and the end of things (Omega). It is God through whom we live, move, and have our being (Acts 17:28). God has made all things, and without Him, nothing was made that is made (John 1:3). God is Triune—there's God the Father, God the Son, and God the Holy Spirit (Matthew 28:19). Finally, I believe it is God the Son, Jesus Christ, who is humanity's only way to get to know and experience the life of God, and thus He is the focus of this book.

You see, Jesus Christ is the central theme of the Bible. Many of the Old Testament stories point to Him or foretell Him before He became a man on earth. The images or scenarios presented in the Old Testament Scripture serve as "types" of Christ; they point forward to a later time when Christ would appear or even further to things that have yet to happen. Jesus Christ emphasized God's heavenly kingdom during His time on earth. He knows it and runs it. He is the Chief Operating Officer (COO) of the Christian faith; it's His way and no other way. And He's done some extraordinary things to earn that rank.

John 3:16 (KJV) says, *For God so loved the world that He gave his only begotten Son, that whosoever believeth in Him should not perish, but have everlasting life.* This is a scripture we had to memorize when I was younger. This verse and other Old Testament feats God performed led me to visualize God and Christ as superheroes. Batman was my favorite superhero, speeding across town in his Batmobile and gliding through the air in his cape to rescue those in trouble or fight crime. Regarding God, as a kid, I'd think, "Wow, God's nice. He loves the entire world? He must be big!" These stories influenced me because kids have active imaginations.

Now, as an adult, I still believe God is big when I look up at how vast the sky is, and think about how it connects all nations, or when I gaze at sunsets, the moon, and stars. My belief in God's greatness is now strengthened because He has shown me that He is big. While Christ is not an imaginary superhero, I have experienced His power. Jesus Christ is real and significant to the Christian faith and the Church. He talks with us, walks with us, and reminds us we're His own; we're a part. We're included in Him.

My Purpose in this Book

My recollections of being unnoticed, experiences, observations, and things I've learned have led to a series of OMG moments in my life. (You'll notice these in the book, where I insert *OMG!* or *Wow*!) These are indicative of times when God amazed me. His attention, love, and care surprised me after I had behaved poorly. Other OMG moments occurred because of erroneous things I've witnessed or experienced in the Lord's Church. (Notice my reference to the Church with a capital "C," signifying the body of Christian believers who are members of Christ's universal church, where there are no branches, denominations, or sects.) Last, I have had a lot of OMG moments (especially today) from the things I read about Jesus Christ or hear in various media that are not supported in Scripture.

Many today are communicating inaccurate, illogical, or incomplete ideas about Jesus Christ. People dilute or misinterpret the message of Jesus Christ. This realization came to me when I compared what is in Scripture with what I'm seeing and hearing. I discovered untruths said about Jesus or minimalizations made of Him. I recognize that Jesus Christ's name is still under scrutiny. He's still misunderstood and misrepresented—even in His Church. This is a deterrent and does not draw people to God, but away from Him. The kingdom of God that Jesus Christ emphasized is uncomplicated and free of chaos, confusion, and conflict.

As a member of Christ's Church, this prompted several questions. "Given that Jesus Christ is the most important figure to the Church, the Christian faith, and our personal lives, why isn't He promoted as such anymore? Why aren't we seeing, hearing, witnessing, or experiencing much of His power? Why is Jesus Christ's mission and message not being taught and passed down?" Compared to the early church (believers in Bible times), people today rarely mention Jesus, misinterpret His message, and have entirely changed His mission for something else.

I questioned further. Why are people turned away from God instead of being brought near to Him? What is Jesus' role in the local church? Is He even there? Have people sidelined Him? Is He on the back burner and only called upon for emergencies? Did we manipulate His agenda and God's plan for sending Him for our own purposes? Given our advancements, ease of life, and our liberties, are we now ashamed of His words and ways? Do we no longer want to do as He did? These are questions I explore in this book, with answers from Scripture. You will learn about Jesus Christ, including His background, His lessons, what He came to do, how He interacted with others, and His relationship with God.

I encourage you to explore Scripture with me, comparing it to how people teach and portray Jesus Christ today. Let's find our errors and return to Jesus as taught in the Bible, making Him the most important thing in our lives, connecting with other Christians, and respectfully sharing Him with the world.

Immanuel Kant was a German philosopher of the Enlightenment period. His family raised him Lutheran, and they stressed religious devotion, humility, and a literal interpretation of the Bible. He changed his views somewhat; however, he said something that captured my attention in college. He stated, "One is not free until he is able to step out of his nonage and apply his reasoning for the masses to hear" (Kant, 1784). What he says here is true. I have stepped out of my nonage, reviewed the Scriptures for myself, and compared them with what I am witnessing about Jesus Christ and the Church, reasoned with God (Isaiah 1:18), and authored this book for the masses to hear. It's a risk.

May Ephesians 1:18-23 (NIV) be your experience after reading it.

I pray that the eyes of your heart may be enlightened in order that you may know the hope to which he has called you, the riches of his glorious inheritance in his holy people, and his incomparably great power for us who believe. That power is the same as the mighty strength he exerted when he raised Christ from the dead and seated him at his right hand in the heavenly realms, far above all rule and authority, power and dominion, and every name that is invoked, not only in the present age but also in the one to come. And God placed all things under his feet and appointed him to be head over everything for the church, which is his body, the fullness of him who fills everything in every way.

Let's go.

Chapter 1 - Salvation in Christ is a Big Deal

Salvation in Jesus Christ stands at the heart of humanity's story—it is the ultimate answer to our deepest problem: the separation from God caused by sin (the word we hate saying or admitting to). Genesis 6:5-6 (NIV) tells us, *The Lord saw how great the wickedness of the human race had become on the earth, and that every inclination of the thoughts of the human heart was only evil all the time. The Lord regretted that he had made human beings on the earth, and his heart was deeply troubled.* So, God takes issue with humanity's ongoing sin.; it's a problem.

The Problem in the Way of Salvation

In the media, we see rescuers—paramedics, police, firefighters, lifeguards—rushing to people in danger to save their lives. The California wildfires are an example. Spreading rapidly, consuming homes and acres of land, we watched intently as firefighters in their heavy protective bunker gear, with hoses in hand, scrambled to stop the fire. They stood for long hours trying to extinguish the flames. Even aerial tankers dropped fire retardant from above, while others used ladders to find and save people. Witnessing their actions, we react: "This is terrible!" Sometimes, watching the devastation makes us cry.

With high adrenaline, rescuers rush into the exact danger that threatens or has harmed the victims. They are intent on saving lives or preserving property. They disregard their own personal safety. Often, rescuers don't know the victims, but they act anyway, knowing the cost could be their own lives. Firefighters brave heat and flames for hours. Police confront gunfire. Lifeguards dive into danger. Their mission: save lives and property.

When people talk about being saved by God, they are alluding to the fact that He has rescued them from something. You ask, "What does salvation or being saved even mean?"

Humanity requires saving. From what? Most don't see the danger we're in or the problem. We think, "I'm okay. My family is fine. I work hard, treat others kindly, and support and give to the less fortunate or important causes." However, this mindset sometimes blinds us. You see, our good deeds and God's provisions don't guarantee a relationship with Him. We face a real danger and need to be saved, as the verse above notes.

The danger started in Eden. God gave the first humans everything they needed to survive. They lived in a perfect environment, enjoying God's provisions: "Go, take, eat," He said. They were free to live and eat as they pleased. But God gave them one command—not to eat from a certain tree. They disobeyed, ate from that tree, and sin entered. Guilt and shame took hold of them, shattering their peace. The garden remained perfect, yet they did not.

An organization I discovered while a student at Colorado Christian University (CCU), The Bible Project, is a crowdfunded project that produces media and other content to help people everywhere experience the Bible as a unified story that leads to Jesus. They explain sin in one of their blogs titled "What Are Sin, Iniquity, and Transgression in the Bible?" You can read it by visiting their main website (https://bibleproject.com/) and searching for the blog title.

See, God is holy and does not sin. Sin separates us from Him and causes a chasm. As made clear in the story of Adam and Eve, God wants us near, to provide for us. However, He takes issue with sin. It troubles and grieves Him because it creates a gap between Him and us. We can't correctly relate to God when sin dominates our lives. When you continue reading the Genesis story, you discover how humans have a natural proclivity to sin; it's our human nature. It controls everyone's life—no matter how good we think we are. God cannot dwell amid sin, be a part of it, or watch our continual struggle with it. The gulf it creates between us aches in His heart—it's intolerable. His longing for closeness is fierce, but we keep spiraling away. The urgency swells. How will a holy God, burdened by burning love, cut through the devastation and save us from ruin.

Unfortunately, this danger is our birthright. As the Genesis verse above reveals, evil works to keep us away from God. The threat lives in our hearts and in the world. (Have you ever noticed how we never give babies lessons in wrongdoing—they just do it by instinct?) "Sin" or "wickedness" describes this inborn tendency. It's the same proclivity to disobey God and commit wrong that Adam and Eve committed in God's perfect garden. Humans have a natural proclivity to sin. We are born in a sinful state and have an instinct, like Adam and Eve, to partake of sin's fruit. Since Adam and Eve's original sin of disobeying God's command not to eat from a particular tree, the verse informs us how sin kept increasing. In fact, man's proclivity for it had gotten so bad that God relented (or regretted) that He had made humankind. That's sad, I'd say. This confirms humanity's condition and how God feels about sin. We recognize it *as* the problem that stands in the way of God and our relating to one another. Sin is why He had to banish Adam and Eve from His perfect garden after they disobeyed Him. Since Adam and Eve's original sin, many generations have come and gone, and sin is still a problem in our world and escalating, right?

If nothing changes, the sorrow persists, passing through time, and God is impassioned to heal the rift with desperation (which He did). For us to relate to God, we first must acknowledge our sinful state; there's no way around this. But He has provided a remedy.

The Remedy

Here's where a savior is key, and Jesus Christ is great to get to know! Jesus Christ is that savior who can rescue us from this condition! He does something for and in us when we accept Him as our Savior. Scripture tells us in Colossians 1:13-14 (NIV), *For he has rescued us from the dominion of darkness and brought us into the kingdom of the Son he loves, in whom we have redemption, the forgiveness of sins.* Jesus Christ accomplished the rescue we all need from sin. Only through Him can we find salvation, which solves the separation we have from God. Acts 4:12 (ESV) reinforces this: *And there is salvation in no one else, for there is no other name under heaven given among men by which we must be saved.*

Emanating from a heart of love and a desire for humanity to be close with Himself, God remedied this sin problem and provided a rescue for us through Jesus Christ. Scripture declares Jesus as "the Savior of the world" (1 John 4:14). He is the one who bridges the gap between God and us, caused by sin, because He has appeased the offense God has against sin. See, sin has a penalty—death—and somebody must pay a price for sin to stay in God's company. Adam and Eve experienced God's penalty—banishment from His perfect presence in the garden. In the Old Testament of the Bible, the Jews had specific rituals they were required to perform to be cleansed of sin; typically, a priest or representative would perform these acts on behalf of the community. But not anymore.

An authentic relationship with God happens by coming to know His Son, Jesus Christ, whom God sent as the remedy to our sin problem. I imagine God whispering to Jesus, *You see, Son? You are the only one who can fix this. There's no other way. You must become the answer. Are you ready?* Jesus did not have this sin problem, as we do. He was perfect, took humanity's sins upon Himself, and satisfied God's righteous requirement. Thus, Jesus bridges the gap between God and us, and only through His sacrifice do we come to know God and experience His life.

Jesus Christ (a good guy) came to earth, lived among us, but for the last time, suffered and died a criminal's death on the cross as payment for our sins. This appeased God and resolved the perpetual sin problem that stands between God and us. Jesus bore the punishment for sin that you and I deserve by shedding His blood. Now, if we believe in Jesus' name as Savior of the world and receive Him as Lord, we are in right standing with God, who considers us righteous. The Bible states this in 2 Corinthians 5:19-21 (NET), *In other words, in Christ God was reconciling the world to himself, not counting people's trespasses against them, and he has given us the message of reconciliation. Therefore, we are ambassadors for Christ, as though God were making his plea through us. We plead with you on Christ's behalf, "Be reconciled to God!" God made the one who did not know sin to be sin for us, so that in him we would become the righteousness of God.* The Easton's Bible Dictionary defines the word reconciling as, "a change from enmity to friendship. It is mutual, i.e., it is a change wrought in both parties who have been at enmity" (Easton's Bible Dictionary). OMG!

Here is the rescue our broken hearts long for, what we need! Sin wells up unbidden in us, threatening to separate us forever from the warmth of God's embrace. We can be close to God by believing in Jesus Christ, who saves us and leads us to a hopeful and righteous life.

"Okay, that makes sense," you surmise. You think, "A savior who can rescue everybody? That is big! Tell me more."

God is not a respecter of persons. He has no favorite race, gender, status, or age group. He does not wish *any* to perish (die before coming to meet Him). So, at some point, He *will* initiate an opportunity for you to come into a relationship with Himself through Christ. He did with me. Don't let your beliefs about God, good qualities, kind nature, religious background, or church attendance prevent you from recognizing God when He appears. The depth of your sinfulness shouldn't bog you down either, or cause you to feel ashamed. Don't allow guilt, shame, or fear to prohibit you from saying "yes" to Him.

You can just come. He's not stacking any cards or counting your sins against you. That's what we humans do. In fact, He's showing up lavished in mercy, forgiveness, and grace. Now, that's an uncomplicated deal you want to make. OMG!

For salvation and to be brought into company with God, receiving His benevolent graces, Jesus is the "OG!" (Ask the younger generation what an "OG" is.) LOL.

Chapter 2 - My Salvation Story

While salvation is a personal journey, unique to everyone, it always leads to one destination: faith in Jesus Christ. The path toward this destination is as diverse as the conditions of our lives. There's no set or uniform way for Jesus to reveal Himself to us and save someone; that's part of the mystery.

Where It Started for Me

My concept of God first took root in the nurturing soil of a Christian home. My maternal family includes a lineage of ministers dating back to 1909. This lineage, this family, was the bedrock of my faith. My mother—a preacher's kid, an evangelist, a preacher, and a children's Bible study teacher—built my spiritual foundation. She influenced me not only in our home but also in the community and the church.

In her womb, I traveled to and from church every Sunday. Sometimes, we went on weekdays as well. I took part in Sunday School, Vacation Bible School, and the Bible clubs she hosted in our home. This was the pattern of my childhood. We try to understand God by reading the Bible, hoping that one day the concept will become reality. We hope one's hearing will turn into believing. That's the understanding my mother had, and that's how it happened to me.

After many years of hearing the Bible, it has shaped what I believe, who I am, and how I choose to live today. But to say I practiced my faith unfailingly would be a lie. Even now, as I write, I have issues—issues you may think disqualify me from authoring this book. Let me save you from wondering. I *don't* qualify to be saved by grace and included as a member of God's family. But I am! All because of what Jesus Christ did on my behalf, I qualify. This realization led me to fall in love with Jesus, His Word, His message, and His ways as I grew and matured.

I love thinking of Him, trying to figure Him out—why He did what He did, the way He said or did things, and how He treated people. I am engaged when I hear the Scriptures taught or preached. Discussions about the Bible or Jesus Christ are exciting to me. The truth about Him astounds me. His stories, His boldness, and His promises move me. Jesus' love keeps my heart beating. His teachings inspired me so much that I earned my degree in biblical studies from Colorado Christian University. I wanted to learn how to communicate His message in a way to help others understand Him better and make His presence real in their lives.

A Family Lineage in Church

I recall those walks to church when I was about seven years old. I also remember the home Bible clubs. Neighborhood children attended Mom's Bible classes or sometimes accompanied us to church. I did not know it, but this nurturing from my early childhood was the beginning of my spiritual journey. The Bible stories captured my interest, prompting questions and sparking further inquiry.

My mother provided the dominant spiritual influence in our home. My dad, too, was a believer and a morally good, respectful man. I believe it was my mother who brought him into a closer relationship with Christ. The lineage of ministers was on her family's side. Her grandfather, Rev. George Winston Porter, founded the First Baptist Church of Darby in 1909. Bishop John Winston Porter, his son, led the Congregational Churches of God in Christ for more than a decade, taking over from the late Bishop Winans. You may be familiar with the gospel recording artist family, the Winans. Long before their fame, my grandfather would return from his trips to Detroit, raving about those "singing boys." How interesting!

My Grandfather, Poppie's Influence

Nothing outweighed his deep affection for his role as Poppie (which we called him) to his thirteen grandchildren born to his son, James Donald Porter, and my mom. Poppie was the love of our lives, not just a seasoned preacher but the greatest granddad any kid could have. He always remembered our birthdays. Each one was special. Our parties weren't complete until we saw him coming down our street or heard his voice at the door. Poppie's beaming smile thrilled us, and we spotted the presents in his hands. We knew there would be wonderful gifts, usually a clothes outfit and plenty of scrumptious candy. Back then, candy came on strings you could loop around your neck like a necklace—lollipops, bubble gum, and candy dots we pulled right off the paper. Poppie would make us stand in front of him while he draped the candy around our necks. We felt like the most special people in the world. Movie stars. Celebrities. He repeated this ritual every year, and did it well, with so much joy. Poppie enjoyed celebrating us. His hugs, kindness, and laughter proved that his love was genuine.

The naps on Poppie's lap also remain a vivid, comforting memory that still soothes me. Nestled in his arms, cheek against his chest, I would drift between sleep and waking, cradled by peace so profound it made the world seem gentle. In his embrace, I felt a security I wouldn't know anywhere else, as if floating in my own private heaven.

Poppie traveled a lot, like a nomad—here one day, then gone for months. He often traveled on the Greyhound bus, visiting churches under his care or his brothers' children on the West Coast. He was the sole connecting point between the East and West Porters in Denver, Colorado, bringing their love back to us. They adored Poppie, too, and called him "Uncle John."

Poppie had an astonishing memory of Scripture, especially the Old Testament. Before preaching, he'd rise, close his eyes, direct congregants to scripture passages, and quote them verbatim. I remember attending his preaching engagements. Even at a young age, I noticed his unconventional methods and delivery. Something inside me knew his sermons broke the rules of church protocol—at least for his denomination and his era. He served where the rules were strict: activities, dress, make-up, and more were challenged or even banned. I teetered on the edge of my seat, elated when Poppie preached. I knew he was teaching something extraordinary and true. He stood and confronted the inequity in the church rules. He was speaking up for the younger generation. Pointing out the contradictions the denomination promoted, he "stirred up the nest," "went against the grain," and it thrilled me. "Yes, Poppie!" I would cheer inside. Of course, I never dared say it out loud. But I knew he was right deep down. Poppie didn't just preach Christ — he showed Him through his care, kindness, and love.

My Mom's Influence

The church ordained my mother, Evangelist Catherine Parks. She carried the same spirit as him. She had his knowledge of the Scriptures, fiery preaching style, and unconventionality. Mom was a true evangelist, first setting the precedent with us at home. There were seven of us—four girls and three boys—Christine, Richard, Carolyn, Judith, Ronald, John, and then the last of the Mohicans, me, Eleanor. All of us participated in the things of God and attended church. Back then, children did not have the option of choosing or bargaining with their parents about attending church. And parents, then, weren't afraid to stand firm and say, "You are going to church, and that's it! End of discussion."

I believe Mom was a true evangelist because evangelists are those who convert souls to the Christian faith (see Ephesians 4:11). Her evangelistic gift revolved around children, where she had the most significant impact. Kids were always in our home and sometimes went with us on fun family outings with Dad. Each week, she taught the Bible to a group of children and offered them an opportunity to receive Jesus Christ as Savior. Her life's work revolved around children. She worked as a teacher and reading aide in the public school system, as a daycare worker for many years, and later opened her own in-home daycare. It's what my mom became known for. She was kind to the children, and they felt loved.

Mom's been gone since 2014, but it amazes me how even now, while walking the neighborhood, taking care of business, or scrolling social media, an adult I do not immediately recognize, if at all, will approach me and ask, "Weren't you in the Bible clubs with Mrs. Parks?" They remember too! The Bible stories stayed with them. Her calling was evident, and she performed it well. At her funeral, several ministers recalled the same route we walked to church with her.

Eventually, my sisters continued hosting the home and community Bible clubs. To me, Chris put the best spin on it; she incorporated puppet shows in the teaching, which the kids loved. She held these both at home and in church buildings, engaging children with stories, games, and prizes. Carol also led clubs, serving kids while pursuing her PhD. Judy is the one who went professional and earned a degree in early childhood education. She taught pre-K children for many years.

As the youngest child, I often watched my siblings teach in the home Bible clubs and at church, but I never took on that role myself. Although Judy once had me fill in for her and teach a club session. I thought it went amazingly well, and Mom and Judy liked it. I was always attentive in the classroom, and it paid off. The seeds of God's word planted in my heart led me one day to recognize Christ's voice and receive Him as my Savior. The Bible went from my head to my heart. Yes, head and heart knowledge differ. I'll share more about that later.

So, it was my mother who instilled in us the reality of God and the importance of living for Him, having compassion for children/people, and inviting others to receive Jesus Christ into their lives as well.

Teenage Years

From my family history, I attended hundreds of church services and took part in many Bible studies throughout my young life. I often had to memorize or quote Scripture. The story of Shadrach, Meshach, and Abednego in the fiery furnace is one of my favorite Bible stories that had me cheering on God and His mighty power. Also, the story of Moses leading the Israelites out of Egyptian bondage was another exciting one to read. When they approached the Red Sea, the Israelites halted because they could not cross over. God instructed Moses to stretch out his rod, and God parted the sea so they could walk over on dry land. "This is phenomenal," I thought! These and other Bible stories are ones that had me imagining God as a superhero.

In my teens and throughout my young adult years, I followed my brother, Ron, a lot. We were closer in age, along with my brother John, the basketball king. The last three children were two boys and me. I attended most churches that Ron did. I could see His life was changing toward the Lord. He became involved in church activities and went to a small Pentecostal church nearby, which had a loving pastor, his wife, and lots of young people. I followed him and got involved too. The younger generation was active there. We sang in the choir, played music, led worship, taught Bible lessons, helped guests, cooked, served food, and worshipped God without inhibition. We also had fun together at church outings, including picnics, roller skating, swimming, and sporting events.

I recall one church picnic when we were playing softball. My turn came up to bat. I hit the ball, flung the bat, and took off running. As I made it to first base, I noticed a crowd gathering around the home plate. I learned I had flung the bat with such force that I had hit one of the church mother's sons in the head with the bat. He had a massive bump on his head. I felt bad, but my energy and enthusiasm did not wane. I continued to have fun at the pool. We were running around the pool, splashing, dunking each other, and playing pool games. The brother of the boy I hit with the bat was standing by the side of the pool. I was an overzealous, tomboyish, and energized teen. Having lots of fun, I see the boy standing on the side. From behind, I sprinted toward the boy and thrust him into the pool. I roared with laughter. Turning around, I thought, "Oh no," as I noticed another crowd had formed! I didn't know, He couldn't swim. I felt terrible once again. My aggression and excitability spoiled these guys' day. Their mother was concerned and pulled me aside, warning me to be careful with her sons. She was not mean about it, though; she was just serious. I got the idea. Ugh! Teenage life.

Anyway, each year at this church, two well-known brothers from New York came to speak. They were impressive teachers and preachers who seemed to bring the spirit of God to their words. The younger generation also enjoyed hearing these brothers. They spoke in a relatable way that we could understand. Their sermons were uplifting and encouraged us to be eager for God.

The brother who came on this particular Sunday taught at an advanced level. He expounded on the Scripture in a relatable way and with emphatic diction. His voice was powerful, and his delivery fiery. Excitement and anticipation filled the air as we prepared. The church would be packed, with no seats available. I was looking forward to hearing his message. "What verse of Scripture will he come from? What life occurrence would he relate it to? Will it be something I need to hear?" I imagined him preaching with such fervor that God's spirit would fall on the congregation like a mighty rushing wind, and we would dance together in praise to God. I liked this Pentecostal fervor. This is what I was anticipating.

Unbeknownst to me, it would not be the preacher or his fervor that would astound me this day. Sitting in my pew, I listened, and the minister did not disappoint. He spoke with passion and fervor. But then something different happened. Something was going on *inside me*. As he concluded his sermon, he began talking about Jesus Christ—who He was, and all He had done for us by dying on the cross for our sins. He told us we needed a personal relationship with Jesus. His message resonated with me, beyond his charisma. I had heard the same message many times before in my family's Bible clubs.

I leaned forward in my seat because his words were piquing my interest. Suddenly, it was as if no one else was in the room and he was talking only to me. I became serious, contemplating the message. My heart began churning inside. I understood what he was saying. Out of nowhere—clearly, softly, and gently — I heard, "This is for you." It was the Holy Spirit speaking to my heart. This message of salvation was for me. The Lord wanted to come into my life. The gentle voice and nudge on my heart were so compelling that when the minister asked the congregation to come to the altar to receive Jesus Christ, I did not hesitate. I knew it was the Lord calling me. I sprang to my feet, walked to the front of the church, and prayed for Jesus Christ to come into my heart as my Lord and Savior. He saved me!

Now, I know what you are thinking; I thought it too. After all I shared about my upbringing, one would think I already knew Christ. Right? I thought so too. Obviously, I did not, because on that day, Jesus' whisper in my ear and tug at my heart assured me I needed to invite Jesus Christ into my life. Understand that in those home Bible clubs, I prayed a salvation prayer—several times. I could have debated God about this and said, "My family already told me about Jesus. I prayed at Bible club and already have Jesus in my life." But I didn't. I *knew* that on this day, something real and different was happening. By my heart's reaction, I *knew* this was a personal knock at the door of my heart, inviting me to believe in and receive Jesus Christ into my life. I *felt* a difference, too.

Jesus Initiates it All

This was a stupendous day when my "superhero," God, revealed Himself to me. Like a perfect gentleman, He started the whole thing, letting me know I needed to be saved. Up to this point, my relationship with God was based on head knowledge. That's okay. Bible club and church attendance were the groundwork that would lead me into a personal relationship with Jesus Christ, where I gave Him my heart. Only Jesus Christ can take our knowledge about the Bible and make it real in our hearts.

I learned something from this experience. Growing up in a Christian environment, like going to church or having a religious family, doesn't mean Jesus is in your life. OMG! Some of you may base your relationship with Jesus on important religious family members, friends, or your moral actions.

Jesus Christ is in your life when you accept His invitation to come into your life. He is in your life when you realize you need Him. He is in your life when you say "Yes" when He calls. In fact, the Scripture teaches us that we can't even come to Christ on our own. It tells us this in John 6:44, *No one can come to me unless the Father who sent me draws them* ... Wow! This is why I said you must say, "Yes," when you sense God's initiative in drawing you.

This is how Jesus Christ saved me, but what is your salvation story? Do you remember? Recall the beauty and profound joy of the day Jesus Christ came into your life. While God approached me in a church service, how He may have saved or will save you is unique to you. Maybe you were alone. Maybe someone talked to you about Jesus in your travels, at work, or in the doctor's office. God chose the Jews as His people "from the gate," not because they were better than other nations, but simply because He is God and can do what He wants. He could have chosen our nation, but He did not. No anger or jealousy toward the Jews; we trust God's sovereignty. With the twelve disciples, He was up close and personal with them, simply telling them to follow. The Lord approached Saul of Tarsus while he was killing and persecuting Christians. Jesus came to him on a road, knocked him to the ground, questioned him about what he was doing, and revealed Himself to him. Saul's name and mission immediately changed from a murderer to one of the greatest evangelists for Jesus Christ. He became Paul.

My mother explained to me how she was saved. Like me, she had heard about Jesus from her father, but she had questions about the truth and embraced several philosophies. Once while in the bathroom, she cried out, "What is the truth; what is the way?" The Lord answered by leading her to the Bible verse found in John 14:6 (NIV), which says, *Jesus answered, I am the way and the truth, and the life. No one comes to the Father except through me.* After that, my mother believed, and Jesus saved her.

Maybe you do not yet have a salvation story. You can. Despite our focus on the problems of teenage and young adult life, the Lord has the power to guide your thoughts and emotions, bringing you to Himself. If you have drifted from your faith and followed the trends of the time, you can return to the Lord. If you think you are too old and set in your ways to find the Lord, you're not.

Regardless of your age or life circumstances, God loves you and wants to rescue you from the penalty of sin. No matter **who you are**, **what you've done**, **when, where, or why you did it**, hear what John 3:16-17 (NIV) is saying to you: *For God so loved the world that he gave his one and only Son, [Jesus Christ] that whoever believes in him shall not perish but have eternal life. For God did not send his Son into the world to condemn the world, but to save the world through him.*

What is this eternal life He is talking about, you may ask? John 17:3 (NIV) tells us, *Now this is eternal life: that they know you, the only true God, and Jesus Christ, whom you have sent.*

Wow! Imagine that! The God of the universe, creator of all things, wants you to know who He and His Son are. OMG!

*** Receive Jesus Christ ***

You may be lying in bed right now with someone who is not your spouse. Or you are coming down from a nice high or are high right now while reading this. Perhaps you are suffering from a hangover. Maybe you're behind bars, facing the consequences of a crime you committed. It's hard to see yourself as being rescued from sin because you are still dealing with it. No worries. Is your heart churning inside you right now? That may be God tapping on the door of your heart to come in. It's okay. Go ahead, open your heart, and let Him rescue you. I wrote a blog titled, "It Only Takes a Taste of Him," based on the Scripture found in Psalm 34:8 (NIV). It simply says, *Taste and see that the Lord is good ...* Just a small sample or taste of Jesus will show you He's good. Go ahead, taste Him, and see!

There is a "Receive Salvation" page is at the end of this book. Follow the steps there for how you can receive Jesus Christ into your life right now.

Chapter 3 - The Blessing in Being Saved

Praise be to the God and Father ... who has blessed us ...

(Ephesians 1:3 NIV)

Maybe you're saying, "Okay, I accepted Jesus Christ into my life, just like you did, but I honestly don't feel any different. Nothing spectacular or mystical happened to me. You say this decision is a big deal, but my life feels the same—it hasn't changed. So, what's next? What else should I do?"

Ephesians 1:1-13

There is a blessing in receiving salvation. When Jesus Christ saves us, a significant change occurs, even if it's not felt all at once. I, like many others, was unaware of the instant change that happens when someone gets saved. Knowing and understanding this sooner can shift the mindset of new Christians; they could "hit the ground running." This chapter helps us see the immediate and life-changing benefits of salvation as described in Ephesians 1:1-13.

Accepting Jesus Christ means God has rescued us from sin and given us a new identity and a place in His kingdom. Our faith in Jesus brings significant benefits. Understanding what these benefits are is crucial to grasping your new life in Christ.

Jesus Christ saved Saul, whom I mentioned earlier, on the Damascus Road while he was persecuting Christians. The Lord renamed him Paul, and after that, he became one of the most important apostles, drafting books like Ephesians that are part of the New Testament. In Ephesians 1:3-13, Paul describes what happens when we accept God's salvation. His letter emphasizes the immediate transformation that took place at our salvation.

In one of his Daily Devotions, entitled "In the Heavenlies," Pastor Ray Stedman writes about these verses in Ephesians. He states, "Obviously, all of this comes to us in one wonderful package in Christ. If you are not a Christian, you cannot possibly claim these benefits, because they are not yours—there is no way you can appropriate them unless you are in Christ. But if you are in Christ, there is nothing to keep you from having all of them, every moment of every day. That is why it is so important that we discover what they are" (Stedman, A Daily Devotional for March 2nd, In the Heavenlies).

The Scripture text starts by addressing the original audience—the 'saints' in Ephesus. It makes a theological statement while also encouraging them. These believers, whom Paul refers to as "the faithful in Christ Jesus," had already received Christ; they were already Christians.

Verse three begins with a praise *to the God and Father of our Lord Jesus Christ…."* Why give Him praise? Paul continues, … *who has blessed us.* The word *"blessed"* here is a Greek word (*eulogeō*) which means "to impart a benefit to someone." Theologian and author Klyne Snodgrass notes how these imparted benefits are not from the physical world but are spiritual blessings proceeding from the heavenly realm. This is the sphere where God resides. He writes, "… 'heavenly realms' does not refer to a physical location but to a spiritual reality—-God's world, in which believers have a share and which evil forces still seek to attack… Though believers live physically on this earth, they receive spiritual resources and their identity from a higher plane… The spiritual blessings given to Christians are enjoyed in the present life, for they derive from what God has done in Christ in the heavenlies." (Snodgrass). Thus, these blessings do not show what will happen in the future, but we received them the moment we put our trust in Jesus Christ. The word "blessed" stated in the past tense helps us realize this has already happened.

Ephesus was a major Roman city known for its temple to Diana (Artemis), one of the Seven Wonders of the World. Artemis's worship affected the city's way of life, including its business practices, which resulted in things like promiscuity, prostitution, witchcraft, and other wrongdoings. These same issues remain common today, don't they?

Paul, with these saints, proclaimed the message of Jesus Christ, united in church fellowship, and taught God's word. This also included new converts, Gentiles, and Greeks, who were turning from their gods to the Lord. The crowd was mixed—longstanding Christians, new Christians, and nonbelievers. He taught them that everyone could now join Jesus Christ and be united by faith. It's no longer just for the Jews. Once alienated from God, the Gentiles are now included because of God's love. Like us, since accepting Him, we are now included and united with God.

In verses 4-13, Paul describes these spiritual benefits. It's important for them to know because these blessings changed their life position, meaning a change in one's status with God. This is now the way they must think and act, not as they once did. These blessings are for *all* the faithful in Christ Jesus. You may think, "I am not really a saint or faithful. I believed in Jesus only recently." Continue reading.

Christians move from spiritual death and separation to being in Christ and accepted by God. We gain a new status—no longer as before.

Reviewing these blessings, we find the word "in" repeated nineteen times, so a definition is warranted. We find the theme of this passage through the use of the terms "in Christ" or "in Him." Snodgrass states, "These are what give this section its power. They are one of the most important components in Paul's theology" (Snodgrass). This signifies that every blessing found here results from being associated with Christ and what He has done. By putting our faith in Jesus Christ, we immediately obtain these blessings from God the Father; they are ours.

7 Blessings Received in Christ

1 **"... Chosen to be holy and blameless..."**

The meaning of this verse is clear. God considers us holy and without fault since we welcomed Jesus. God's perspective on us stems entirely from our connection to Christ. We might act holy if we're reminded that God sees us this way.

"... predestined us to be adopted as his sons through Jesus Christ..."

Predestination means God decided before He formed the world and before we were born, to choose us as children in His family. To think the God of the universe had you and me in mind to accept us as His children! 2

3 **"... We have redemption through his blood ..."**

Remember the penalty for sin deserved death? A sacrifice was necessary to prevent that penalty. Jesus Christ paid that penalty by shedding His blood and dying on the cross. From God's viewpoint, Jesus' blood was enough payment to cover you and me. Now, through our faith in Jesus' blood, God passes over the penalty we deserve because Christ paid it in full, once for all.

"... the forgiveness of sins in accordance with the riches of God's grace ..." 

God is so rich in grace (undeserving favor toward us) that through Christ's sacrificial death, He would bridge this gap between our sinfulness and God's righteous requirement. He lavishes in forgiveness, and we are forgiven of our sinful condition and receive forgiveness daily as we confess to Him.

5 **"...made known to us the mystery of his will according to his good pleasure..."**

Why is this a blessing? Well, it denotes how we are now no longer strangers to God. As members now of His family, we are heirs with God and joint heirs with Christ (Romans 8:17 NIV). As His children, now God shares classified information with us, information that was once hidden. One day He will bring all things in heaven and earth under one head.

"…. we were also chosen, having been predestined according to the plan of Him who works out everything in conformity with the purpose of His will..."

Christians do not live life aimlessly. God had a predetermined plan for choosing us. He will work out all things to conform to His will that would bring Him glory. This includes our good, our bad, and our ugly.

"…. you were marked in Him with a seal, the promised Holy Spirit, who is a deposit guaranteeing our inheritance until the redemption of those who are God's possession..."

At our conversion, we receive a "seal" and a "deposit" – the promised Holy Spirit. His mark validates us as one of God's own and serves as a down payment or guarantee of our place in heaven. In Christ, God puts His stamp of approval on us to walk through the pearly gates! 7

How blessed we are, eh! These blessings in Christ are life-changing—they unveil our new status with God now and in the future. They reveal God's wisdom and the care, love, mercy, grace, and generosity that He is full of and lavishes on us, with no strings attached.

It's important that new Christians learn about these blessings after conversion so they can reflect on them regularly. The core message is that these blessings form the foundation of your new identity in Christ. They empower new ways of thinking and acting while giving you confidence in your relationship with God. They are not based on how we may feel after receiving Christ, although knowing about them may affect how we feel.

So, the question becomes, are we teaching this in Christ's Church today? Do we even know this truth? Or are we demanding new Christians follow church protocol as opposed to teaching them what Jesus Christ afforded them? Imagine the impact if every new Christian learned these truths right after receiving Jesus Christ—wouldn't it encourage them?

Reflecting on these blessings given to us at salvation helps us form a better view of God. Understanding them would inspire us to act differently, in accordance with how God now sees us. Wouldn't we be more likely to act in a holy manner if we knew that God now sees us as holy? Knowing these blessings can increase our self-esteem. Meditating on these blessings would remove doubt and fear during trials so we don't shrink back, just as Paul and the Ephesians didn't. Most importantly, we would realize how much God cares about us and accepts us—all because we put our faith in His Son.

Faith in Jesus gives us a new identity, and these blessings are yours. These aren't blessings you have to work for to earn. If you feel unworthy, ask God to remove any barriers prohibiting you from believing these blessings are for you. Let go of your doubts and embrace God's acceptance, His lavish nature to give to us. Ask Him to remove any negative assessments about yourself that came from others—family, friends, the law, psychiatrists, social media, coworkers, neighbors, teachers, your ex, or whoever.

Let's close with a prayer from Ephesians 1:15-23 (ESV). May the Lord help you believe these truths, embrace your new identity, and live as God sees you. Let these truths shape your life and guide you in faith and purpose.

We begin,

Praise to the God and Father of our Lord Jesus Christ. For this reason, because I have heard of your faith in the Lord Jesus and your love toward all the saints, I do not cease to give thanks for you, remembering you in my prayers, that the God of our Lord Jesus Christ, the Father of glory, may give you the Spirit of wisdom and of revelation in the knowledge of him, having the eyes of your hearts enlightened, that you may know what is the hope to which he has called you, what are the riches of his glorious inheritance in the saints, and what is the immeasurable greatness of his power toward us who believe, according to the working of his great might that he worked in Christ when he raised him from the dead and seated him at his right hand in the heavenly places, far above all rule and authority and power and dominion, and above every name that is named, not only in this age but also in the one to come. And he put all things under his feet and gave him as head over all things to the church, which is his body, the fullness of him who fills all in all. Amen.

OMG! What a deal! Wall Street can't match God's wealth and riches.

Chapter 4 - Don't Just Take My Word; It's in the Bible

All Scripture is God-breathed and is useful for teaching, rebuking, correcting, and training in righteousness, so that the servant of God may be thoroughly equipped for every good work.

(2 Timothy 3:16-17 NIV)

What value is there in a relationship where only one person puts in the effort? I'm usually the initiator in my relationships, asking questions, giving advice, or making suggestions. Most of my friends didn't seem interested in my ideas or wanted to do something else. As a result, I learned to do things alone — a skill my mom taught me: "Learn to entertain yourself." Maybe I was weird to them, since what interested me rarely appealed to others. Or were they genuine friends? Perhaps not. These revelations are not always apparent at first; they come in time.

If we don't cultivate a relationship—new or old—what's the use? Why are we in it? The relationship will eventually become a stalemate. It's going nowhere, and both of you will remain in the same state, the same place, where nothing new is happening. There's no growth. Relationships grow stronger when people attempt to hone them, either by spending time together or by communicating. Shared activities—a walk in the park, dining, binge-watching TV, or working out—help us learn each other's ways. Without cultivation, relationships stagnate and cannot grow. I have always believed that relationships, especially romantic ones, should bring out the best in you.

The same applies in our relationship with God the Father through His Son, Jesus Christ. To grow, we must cultivate it. He accepts us into His family, even though we were once far from Him. God forgives our sins—past, present, and future—and sees us as righteous. The Holy Spirit sealed this relationship when we believed the message of Jesus Christ; it can never be broken, and we should not abandon it. We can now draw near to Him.

When we first meet Jesus Christ, we don't know God's ways or what His kingdom is like. We're accustomed to our earthly experience. Most of what we do, our way of thinking, and how we respond to situations, is shaped by our earthly existence. God, on the other hand, is Spirit and lives in a heavenly realm. So, can we cultivate our relationship with Him? How can we come to know Him more deeply and represent Him in the correct way? Where do we go to learn more about Jesus and the Christian life? Should we attend church, follow other Christians, pray and wait for answers, or just continue life as usual and figure things out on our own?

Well, the answer is both yes and no. Remember, Jesus Christ initiated this relationship with us to bring us to God. Now, God isn't hiding any secrets from us about His ways or His kingdom, as we learned in Ephesians. Recall from John 17 that eternal life means knowing God and His Son. Clearly, God wants us to know Him better. This prompts important questions: What is God's nature? What is His kingdom, and how does it operate? What does it mean for God to reveal Himself as three persons — God the Father, God the Son, and God the Holy Spirit—while still being one? How do these three exist separately but together? You may have other questions you want answered about God as well.

As members now of God's family, we should want to know who He is, what He's like, what He does, and how He thinks and operates. We touched on Jesus' unique importance to the Father and their connection. We now understand Jesus' role in salvation, but what else makes Him significant? Who is Jesus as a whole? How was He on earth? These questions matter—and we can find answers. Jesus is no longer visible, but He made a lasting impact. There is a place to learn about Him—a place where God has revealed Himself. Instead of relying on guesses or others, we must engage with Scripture. By centering our faith on the Bible, we can discover who God is, what His kingdom is like, and how to represent Him. This is the foundation of authentic Christian growth. The Bible is the primary source of Christian truth. Many Christians do not read Scripture, often because of a lack of awareness or guidance; yet, reading Scripture is essential for knowing God. This practice is essential for a genuine relationship with Him.

In an article by Ed Stetzer, Executive Director of LifeWay Research Division, entitled "The Epidemic of Bible Illiteracy in Our Churches," he notes how, "Christians claim to believe the Bible is God's Word. We claim it's God's divinely inspired, inerrant message to us. Yet despite this, we aren't reading it. A recent LifeWay Research study found that only 45 percent of those who regularly attend church read the Bible more than once a week. Over 40 percent of the people attending read their Bible occasionally, maybe once or twice a month. Almost 1 in 5 churchgoers say they never read the Bible—essentially the same number who read it every day" (E. Stetzer).

These statistics highlight a key point: many who claim to follow Jesus Christ rarely follow the Bible, the essential source for knowing Him. To strengthen our faith and relationship with God, regular engagement with Scripture is necessary.

I would argue further that as professed followers of Jesus Christ, we can't ignore, neglect, dispute, or deny the Bible's relevance to our lives. Personally, I did not always read or study the Scriptures outside church settings. When I did or heard it preached during a sermon or in class, sometimes I was confused; I struggled to understand its meaning. I'd think, *"What is this talking about? I don't get it."* Do you feel this way? To understand God and grow as followers of Christ, we need to read the Bible. Life in Christ is not a competition or about achievement; the goal is a transformed life. We don't strive in the Christian faith. Receiving Jesus makes us whole, shifting our focus to knowing Him through Scripture rather than striving by worldly means.

Americans are groomed to thrive, work hard, and pursue the "American Dream." For a while, I applied these cultural values to my faith, approaching my relationship with Jesus Christ in the way my culture had groomed me. I know I'm not alone here; it's common among Christians. I hear it. This may explain why many struggle to find peace and feel upset and unsettled in their spirit. We strive to change habits, live godly lives, and treat people right. The Lord showed me I was a striving Christian. I often thought, "I've got to get this right," or "I must work harder and do better next time." Most days, I experienced stress! OMG!

A proper understanding of Jesus Christ, found in the Bible, ends this striving mentality. Jesus promised His followers a "rest." Without apparent knowledge of Him from Scripture, we risk being led astray. We become vulnerable, like wandering sheep, and are open to anything that delights our senses or that can convince us. That's why reading the Bible is vital to our faith. There is significant evidence, from both experience and other sources, that the Bible is vital for Christian life. By reading and studying the Bible, we can find the truth about Jesus, keep our faith strong, and avoid being misled.

From the Old Testament to the New, the Bible centers on Jesus Christ. In its pages, you will find types of Jesus revealed in Old Testament stories, prophecies about His coming, and messages written by those close to Him. These prophecies foretell His coming as the Messiah, telling where He would be born, what He would do, and how He would suffer. Jesus also made claims about who He is in the Bible. When you begin to "connect the dots," it's fascinating!

Dr. Craig A. Carter confirms this in his book, "Interpreting Scripture with the Great Tradition: Recovering the Genius of Premodern Exegesis." He writes: "The authority of the Bible is God's self-authenticating Word speaking through it, and in order to hear God's Word, it is crucial that we interpret it as a unified book with Jesus Christ at its center" (Carter).

The Bible contains a wealth of truth about Jesus Christ. So, it's essential to gain an interest in reading the Bible, whether or not you are a Christian, or if you are just researching Jesus. Why rely only on the Bible rather than on a movie depiction, documentary, or informative book (as good as they may be) about Jesus? The Bible is the document through which God reveals Himself to us. His truth. In it, we learn about God's nature, the doctrines of the Christian faith, and the life of Jesus Christ. The Bible *is* God's source of communication to us.

It is in Scripture that we obtain the truth about God's Son, Jesus Christ, and His significance to the Father, the Christian faith, our personal lives, the Church, and the world. God has spoken through His Son, Jesus Christ. Hebrews 1:1-2 (NIV) states, *In the past God spoke to our ancestors through the prophets at many times and in various ways, but in these last days He has spoken to us by His Son, whom He appointed heir of all things, and through whom also He made the universe.* Here, we see the importance God has placed on observing Jesus Christ. Jesus Christ is heir to God's throne.

We discover in this verse of scripture that God is no longer speaking as He once did in times past—through the prophets, such as Moses, David, and Elijah. Now, in sending Christ, He has sent humanity another message. So, if someone tells you they have a message from God, take a moment to consider it, but recall this is not God's primary way now of communicating with us. Second in this verse, it's important we learn about Jesus Christ as God's heir. An heir inherits everything that belongs to the owner of something. We hear stories in the news about celebrities or wealthy persons' children inheriting their parents' estates. Everything in the parents' estate now belongs to the kids; they control everything in it and can manage it any way they choose. So, it is with Christ. He has inherited the rank, title, and position of God. In His actions, He showed us what God, the Father, is like and represented Him perfectly. He now rules and manages the affairs of God's kingdom.

Last, the verse illustrates how Jesus has always been, despite humans not knowing about Him until He was born on earth. When God formed the universe, this Bible verse reveals that Christ was present and a part of that process. Thus, we can ascertain that Jesus Christ is important to God the Father and, therefore, important to read about and study.

What Biblical Scholars Say About the Bible

Author Millard Erickson helps us understand the reasoning behind the Bible's importance. In his book, *Introducing Christian Doctrine*, he writes, "God is the ultimate authority in religious matters. He has the right, both by virtue of who He is and what He does, to establish the standard for belief and practice. With respect to major issues, He does not exercise authority in a direct fashion, however. Rather, He has delegated that authority by creating a book, the Bible. Because it conveys His message, the Bible carries the same weight God Himself would command if He were speaking to us personally" (Erickson 77).

Another author I learned about while studying at CCU also testifies to the Bible's importance. In his book, "The Unfolding Mystery: Discovering Christ in the Old Testament," Edmund Clowney writes, "The Bible is the greatest storybook, not just because it is full of wonderful [fictional] stories but because it tells one great story, the story of Jesus... The story is God's story" (Clowney 11,13). I agree that the stories recorded in the Bible are God's stories about His beloved Son, Jesus Christ, who would save humanity from their sins. It was imperative, then, that God delivered His message in the original language of the people at that time and for that culture—Israel. Thank God, we now have professional translators who can accurately translate Scripture texts from their original languages—Hebrew, Aramaic, and Greek — into English, allowing us to better understand what God is saying.

Karl Barth is another well-known theologian I appreciate. After reading his Twelve Theses about the Bible, I saw he wanted to show the importance of the Bible's authority throughout time. He writes, "Its significance is for God's people Israel—in times past, the apostles/prophets in the dispensation of Christ, and for the salvation of the world—to future generations who would read or hear about it," (Barth). Barth also emphasizes "how the authority and significance of the Bible make for God's establishment of a relationship with people. Humankind receives God's word, witnesses God's word, and receives salvation through God's word. Having this authority and significance, the Bible stands as the only word that reflects the nature, character, and ways of God. It is the truth that brings life to those who would receive it and guidance, comfort, and healing to one's soul. The authority and significance of God's word stand as the church's only guide in spiritual matters" (Barth).

I agree with Barth where he says, "God's word stands as the church's only guide in spiritual matters." It should be this way. However, I question whether this is the case today when we examine the affairs going on in the local church. What message is being communicated? What is the current state of the church's operations? More importantly, is God's relational aspect highlighted, or is affiliation with a church building, its protocol, and reverence for its leaders the emphasis? Are we turning people away from Jesus and more toward acclimation with people? The church appears to be more of a performance, social club, and entertainment venue, where leading actors take the stage.

If Christians believe the Bible is their sole spiritual guide, why do the statistics on Bible reading seem so low? The Church *must* adopt this perspective on the authority, relevance, and importance of the Bible. Since they represent God's Kingdom with Christ as leader, Christians must follow the Bible instead of political or cultural ideas. Jesus shows us in the Bible how His culture, family, and neighborhood of origin all took second place to God's kingdom and His mission. We, too, should change our cultural perspectives, political ideologies, and allegiance to our country of origin to the Bible's stance on matters of life, death, and social and global issues. This isn't always easy to do at first. We cannot align ourselves with people or organizations and speak their message that is counterintuitive to Christ's way. This is the challenge Jesus endured.

It's crucial to our faith, how we live in the world, and how we relate to others in society. A biblical worldview reveals God. Having a biblical worldview helps us understand Jesus Christ as the preeminent One in the Bible. We will want to emulate Him. There is no other place that promulgates the significance, authority, and lordship of Jesus Christ, except the Bible. The prophets and writers of the Old and New Testaments witnessed and spoke of the Holy Spirit, who establishes and confirms God's word. (More about the Holy Spirit is coming.)

What the Biblical Authors Say About Jesus Christ in the Bible

The Old Testament books of the Bible foretold Jesus Christ before He arrived. Genesis through Malachi includes the Old Testament. The Israelites spread and shared these prophecies about the Messiah for ages. Prophets of old knew about the coming Messiah. There are also Old Testament characters and things they experienced in the stories that serve as types of Christ. For example, in the Israelite community, a story is told about a Pharaoh who came after the Israelite community to kill all the firstborn of Israel. Moses had them spread blood over their doorposts so death would pass by their homes, and all the firstborns would live. The act of spreading blood was a symbol of what Christ's blood would achieve for us—save us from sin's penalty—death — and eternal separation from God.

Another type of Christ in the Old Testament relates to how the Israelites were to be cleansed of sin to relate with God. The priests had to present a spotless lamb to atone for the sins of the community. This too is a type of Christ. When Jesus began His public ministry, He declared Himself to be the Lamb of God, who would take away the sins of the world. (See John 1:29.) No longer would this sacrificial ritual need to be performed by a priest; Jesus, the Lamb of God, would do it with His blood, one time for all. Isn't this remarkable?

Then, there are the New Testament authors. Those who were close to Jesus and wrote about their experience, or told others what they knew, and those people also wrote about Him. Once Jesus was gone, the apostles, or his main followers, started teaching and forming the Christian church, spreading from Judea to every corner of the earth. When you read the New

Testament, you will notice how the authors always point to Jesus Christ in their messages to the people. They acknowledge and exalt Him as the preeminent One and not themselves. In fact, you will notice their self-effacement to give Jesus Christ all the glory.

Scholars classify Matthew, Mark, and Luke as the synoptic gospels, while they separate the book of John because it presents a distinct narrative structure and style. John focuses more on Jesus' divinity and his unique relationship with God. The three are synoptic because they share similar stories that record Jesus' life and ministry, as well as the words He spoke while on earth. These writings came from Jesus' disciples and others. Mark and Luke received the message from them. Paul, who is the most important writer in the New Testament, wrote letters, or epistles, to the first churches. These letters also support what Christ said about Himself and what they had heard, seen, experienced, or were told.

Some of these men were eyewitnesses to what Jesus did, how He lived, and the miracles He performed. So, we should trust the biblical authors' messages. Who can tell a story better than an eyewitness who was there, live and in color? They deserve our respect, and we should listen to them. Their letters were situational or occasional and written to Christians to address a specific issue and/or meet a particular need.

These biblical authors record Christ as being: *the future Judge* (John 5:22-23); *the Lamb of God* (John 1:36); *the baptizer in the Holy Spirit* (Luke 3:16); *the door of salvation* (John 10:9); *the Savior* (John 3:14-16); *the Messiah* (John 4:26); *the healer* (Luke 18:42); *the Son of God* (Matthew 26:63); and *the Son of Man* (Matthew 16:13; Mark 14:62). Where did they get this information? From Christ Himself, through what they witnessed, through the Holy Spirit, or from an Old Testament prophecy told centuries ago.

What Jesus Said about Himself in the Bible

Jesus, too, made several "I am" statements about Himself in the Bible. They are bold and emphatic statements we would be wise to learn about the Christ we follow. These are claims Jesus made that often confused the crowds, angered the religious establishment, and got Jesus in big trouble. When His haters surfaced, when doubts arose, or when He faced threats, He did not retract or change them. Jesus said about Himself:

- **"I am the Way, and the Truth, and the Life;** no one comes to the Father, but through Me" (John 14:6).

Jesus asserts here that He is the way to God, the truth, and the life.

- "**I am the bread of life**" (John 6:35, 41, 48, 51).

  Here, Jesus asserts He offers and sustains spiritual life.
- "**I am the light of the world**" (John 8:12).

  Here, Jesus asserts to a world lost in darkness that He guides us into the light.
- "**I am the door of the sheep**" (John 10:7, 9).

  Jesus asserts how He protects His followers as shepherds protect their flocks from predators.
- "**I am the resurrection and the life**" (John 11:25).

  Jesus asserts His power over death and life.
- "**I am the good shepherd**" (John 10:11, 14).

  Here, Jesus asserts His goodness in caring for and watching over His followers.
- "**I am the true vine**" (John 15:1, 5).

  Here, Jesus asserts Himself as the true vine, who, if we remain attached to, will cause us to bear fruit that honors God.

Also, while teaching in the temple, standing on a mountain, or healing the multitudes of people in the streets or by a sea, Jesus referred to Himself as: **the giver of eternal life** (John 10:28); **One with the Father** (John 10:30); **One who forgives sin** (Mark 2:10); the **great "I Am"** (John 8:58); and the **giver of living water** (John 4:10). You can read these and other claims Jesus made in the Bible in your own time. They reveal Jesus' character and the authority He possessed.

I hope you are seeing why Jesus was so extraordinary and is important to get to know and understand! There's more to Him than meets the eye.

What Critics Say About the Bible

As with any influential book or writing, there are always those who read it as critics, intending to offer opinions that contradict, dispute, or challenge it, or to discredit the work altogether. Over the centuries, many discourses about the Bible have emerged. We hear people trying to discredit the Bible's authenticity and/or relevance. People I've talked with don't trust the Bible because they think too many people have changed it over the years, while it was being passed down. "It's not trustworthy," they say. Also, some filmmakers create documentaries that point out inconsistencies in the Bible, such as issues with Jesus' travels and differing historical records. They analyze the inconsistencies found in the dates, times, or facts presented in Scripture.

These naysayers often lack information, present illogical arguments, or make an incomplete analysis when arguing against the Bible or Jesus Christ. One of the first things I learned in my study of the Bible at CCU was how we should *not* approach reading the Bible. One must have a clear and open mind, able to put aside one's own viewpoints, presuppositions, opinions, or biases when reading it. Next, use hermeneutical principles (the practice of interpretation) that guide us from the historical meaning of the scriptures to their meaning for today.

Brian Auten, retired founder of Apologetics 315, writes, "Good books are imperative for learning and growing. However, many people read their good books at random. Sporadic reading may have the small benefit of keeping you interested as you jump from topic to topic — but one problem can be that often the information hasn't saturated your mind long enough for you to ruminate on that subject over an extended period" (Auten). Learning what the Scripture is saying and understanding it takes time; we need the Holy Spirit's help. We cannot read the Bible as above, and you can't patch together passages of Scripture just to support your view on something.

Christian belief holds that God is the inspiration for the contents of His written word, where He used biblical authors to convey His message. Thus, we hold the Bible to be God's message to humanity. God's transcendence, goodness, and perfection substantiate the truth. Men wrote as God inspired them. We believe the record of Christ's earthly ministry is dependable. The epistles and messages of the Old and New Testaments are those that God the Father intended for humanity to know. God's direction has not included Thomas' gospels and others that they discovered. Just as we believe the Holy Spirit inspired the writing of Scripture, we should also believe the Holy Spirit protected it. To emphatically suggest that the biblical authors did not agree with one another may support one's reasoning for concluding that it is faulty or illogical; however, you should understand that some of these arguments and documentarians have one ulterior motive: they simply do not believe the message of the Bible.

It's natural to encounter criticism, be put on blast, and receive negative views on any written work. Putting people on blast is, in fact, the trend in our day. Criticism is something we should address or discuss only with the truth of Scripture, not fight over.

Christians believe in the Bible's inerrancy. The passage in the Bible that settles all these matters (for me) and inspires my thinking about these negative views on the Bible is 2 Peter 1:20-21 (NIV). It says, *Above all, you must understand that no prophecy of Scripture came about by the prophet's own interpretation of things. For prophecy never had its origin in the human will, but prophets, though human, spoke from God as they were carried along by the Holy Spirit*. It's clear from this scripture that the prophets did not include their interpretation when they wrote the sacred Scriptures. The biblical authors did not draw words from their imaginations or invent fictional stories. Their words didn't even arise from their superior intellect. They wrote as the Holy Spirit spoke to them. Thus, putting the decisive weight of authorship on God's side would prove the strength, infallibility, inerrancy, and truth of God's word. Christians should believe that in the narrative stories of the Old and New Testaments, there are no weaknesses in putting the decisive weight in the Bible's writing on God's side.

We also believe the Bible is infallible; it's incapable of making mistakes or being incorrect. When we discuss the Bible's infallibility, Charles Hodge attributes the Bible's infallibility directly to the Holy Spirit's work through the sacred writers. For Hodge, biblical infallibility meant that the original manuscripts were incapable of error, and this was a necessary consequence of divine inspiration. He believed that God's divine superintendence ensured the truth of both the thoughts and words of the biblical writers. He states, "The Scriptures of the Old and New Testaments are the Word of God, written under the inspiration of the Holy Spirit, and are therefore infallible, and of divine authority in all things pertaining to faith and practice, and consequently free from all error whether of doctrine, fact, or precept" (Battle 17:27).

Regarding the Bible as revelation, theologian Alister McGrath defines revelation as "... removing a veil so that something can be revealed... The minds, hearts, imaginations, consciences, and wills of men were used, but the Scriptures are nevertheless in the strictest sense the word of God. The divine influence of the Holy Spirit upon what the writers wrote was demonstrated in their expression of their thoughts in language, as well as their own thoughts... These thoughts reflected with infallibility the exact message God wanted to convey" (McGrath 228-229)Wow! This is important, folks. Our faith in the greatness of God and His almighty power (God is big, remember?) to carry this out should dispel any doubts when we hear or are challenged by others on the credibility of the Bible, because we're assured it is God's communication to us, drawing us closer to Him. We conclude, then, that if God wrote it, God said it, and that settles it!

Conclusion

If Christians don't see the Bible as the only spiritual authority, or we have trivialized it, or eliminated the Holy Spirit's role in understanding it, who or what then *are* we listening to and relying upon in understanding, interpreting, teaching, preaching, or sharing it with others? OMG! Consider these questions to identify any blind spots you may have in your view of the Scriptures. Place a check mark where you struggle, then commit it to God.

- Are we proclaiming Jesus Christ, the Messiah in the Bible, or a movie depiction of Him?
- Is the Bible our only go-to place in an age of technological advancements, where now so much information is freely circulating at the speed of light?
- Have we omitted the importance of God's word for guiding our lives and teaching others?
- Does the Bible shape our worldview? Are we addressing global issues or advising and counseling people through a biblical lens?
- Do we understand Christ through our cultural worldview?
- Have we diluted the power of the Gospel message and tarnished it by mixing in worldly concepts, ideologies, or ideas?
- Have we replaced or ignored the Holy Spirit's role in our understanding of Scripture?
- Have we disqualified the biblical authors' message or tried to supersede their witness?
- Are our presuppositions, reasonings, biases, and imaginations controlling the Bible narrative?

A Lamp for My Feet

Psalm 119:105 talks about how God's word is a lamp for our feet and a light to our path. (The same thing Jesus claims to be.) I am not fond of coming home to a dark house. I must leave a lamp on when I go out and know I won't be returning until it's dark. This is to ensure that everything is clear when I enter. I don't want to trip or stub my toe on a coffee table. I also like to peruse my house to ensure no intruders have entered and nothing is out of place. According to this verse, this is true of what God does for us through His Word. God's word lights the path and makes clear the way we should walk. The Bible shows us the path God wants us to take so we will not stumble, fall, and hurt ourselves along the way. It exposes intruders and enemy action that are contrary to God's kingdom life. OMG!

Surely then, it is wise to pick it up and start reading—even if you don't understand what it is saying. Keep reading; soon you will. The dots will connect, and you will begin learning about and understanding your friend, Jesus, a lot better

Chapter 5 - The Earthly Jesus, aka The Son of Man

Here's where learning the facts about Jesus Christ, the man, is exciting. If you're a first-time Bible reader or new to hearing about Him, follow along.

Once, while talking with Nicodemus, a religious leader uncertain about spiritual matters, Jesus identifies Himself as the "Son of Man" (John 3:13). This title shows that Jesus was human and the Messiah, connecting Him to people and hinting at His role. He is also called "the one who came from heaven." The title appears in Daniel 7:13-14, describing a figure with God-given power, glory, and authority—a ruler. Interesting, a human who came from heaven!

It's fascinating to me that God—who exceeds time and space and is immanent (meaning present in all creation yet remains distinct from it)—chose to send His beloved Son, Jesus Christ, into our sphere of life (earth) by natural means like other humans. This action leads us to a central question: Why did Jesus, who was "living large" and at peace in the heavenlies, consent to come into our zone of existence? He would have to leave all His heavenly glory. Could you tell me why God would send His beloved only Son to dwell among us, lowly creatures? The Bible tells us why. Let's move to the answer.

Recall our earlier discussion about rescuers who will face the same danger as those they help. This is what Jesus Christ did. He left His beautiful, non-chaotic heavenly home to experience life among us. Hebrews 4:15-16 (NIV) says of Jesus: *For we do not have a high priest who is unable to empathize with our weaknesses, but we have one who has been tempted in every way, just as we are—yet he did not sin. Let us then approach God's throne of grace with confidence, so that we may receive mercy and find grace to help us in our time of need.*

Isn't this remarkable! Jesus Christ relinquished His glory, came to earth as a man to walk among us, and experienced the same things we experience. Because He did, He now can understand and relate to us. He can sympathize and empathize with our human weaknesses because He's been there. He knows all the temptations, struggles, and pain we encounter as humans because He too experienced them. (More about His struggles are upcoming.)

This scripture invites us, then, to pray to God without fear, and we will receive His mercy and grace when we need it most. We can do this because Jesus understands our weaknesses, our struggles; He had them as well. There is no need for hesitation or shame when we bring our concerns to God. The same help that supported Jesus is available to us.

Jesus Christ is a great high priest and can help us because He endured human frailties, trials, and temptations. What distinguishes Him from us is what the verse tells us, *but He has been tempted in every way just as we are, yet without sin.* Jesus did not mess up like we do, take revenge, or curse people out when they hurt Him. He was victorious through every trial, every hurt, every temptation, and every betrayal. He never sinned, completely satisfied God, and therefore qualified as "a great High Priest" who can offer us help on how we too can make it through life's challenges. Isn't that outstanding?

The Man, Christ Jesus

Jesus was born into a race of people, lived in a community with cultural and legal systems, and a family raised Him, just like all of us. The New Testament gospels—Matthew, Mark, Luke, and John — are the only books in the Bible that contain details about Jesus' life. Let's avoid debate and look at the simple biblical message about Jesus Christ's earthly life.

Messianic Prophecies about Jesus Christ

As said earlier, before Jesus Christ was born, people in the Jewish community wrote and shared prophecies about Him. Understanding what the prophets spoke about Jesus Christ thousands of years before He was born is essential. As we continue our study, we will see how Jesus fulfilled most of these prophecies when He came to earth. In Chapter 4, we read Hebrews 1:1 (NIV), which says: *"In the past God spoke to our ancestors through the prophets."* God spoke to them about Jesus Christ as the coming Messiah. The prophecies should help the Jews recognize Jesus Christ when He appears. Did they recognize Him? Some did; some did not. Some rejected Him because they did not agree with the way He came.

A Bible prophecy is God's inspired words about future events, delivered through prophets. These prophecies can predict what will happen, share divine knowledge, and offer people advice and help. They are predictions that come true, warnings about what is coming, or promises from God about grace and salvation.

The Christianity.com editorial staff helps us understand. They write, "The term 'prophecy' in the Bible encapsulates the divine communication of God's will, often foretelling future events or conveying messages of moral and spiritual significance. Prophets, as designated messengers of

God, play a pivotal role in the dynamic relationship between the Creator and His creation. The voices of prophets such as Moses or Elijah, and Isaiah echo through the pages of the Old and New Testaments, each prophet uniquely contributing to the unfolding story of salvation, redemption, and the fulfillment of God's promises," (Christianity.com).

There are many self-proclaimed "prophets" in the Christian Church today. I don't know why, but it's a coveted title, along with the title of apostle. You hear on TV or read on social media, people proclaiming themselves as Prophet or Apostle so and so. Some may truly be, but some have taken this gift of prophecy and the act of prophesying to others out of context and misappropriated it. They haven't brought people closer to God, but instead have caused more disappointment, confusion, and pain. Allow me to apologize if someone in the name of "prophet" lied to, misinformed, misjudged, or hurt you; this was not God. Most times, people use the title or position for self-glorification. People are told things in the name of God to make the "prophet" appear divine or special. They claim mysterious close encounters with God, making others view them as untouchable and worthy of respect. In fact, Paul urged Christians to "eagerly desire the greater gifts," and then guides them to the most excellent way of them all—love. (I said we wouldn't debate here.) Let's continue explaining this gift.

Christianity.com continues that, "Prophecy, at its most fundamental meaning, is 'a message from God.' Hence, to prophesy is to declare a message from God. Let's look at the definition for each for more clarification: Prophecy: *Noun* "a prediction; the faculty, function, or practice of prophesying." Prophesy: *Verb* "to utter by or as if by divine inspiration; to predict with assurance or on the basis of mystic knowledge. In short, we can describe prophecy as the message and prophesy as delivering that message" (Christianity.com).

Author Dr. Henrietta Mears informs us that the ancient prophets were not just talking to be talking. They were not just announcing or predicting anything about Jesus Christ. There was a particular message God wanted to convey. In her book, "What the Bible is All About," she notes, "The prophets have portrayed a magnificent picture of the Messiah. They have told of his offices, mission, birth, suffering, death, resurrection, and glory" (Mears 367).

The infographics below lists some of the Messianic prophecies made about Jesus Christ *before* He came into the world. It includes the Old Testament scripture verse and the New Testament verses that show when Jesus Christ fulfilled them

MESSIANIC PROPHECIES OF JESUS CHRIST			
Prophecy	**Old Testament Scripture**	**Summary**	**New Testament Fulfillment**
The Messiah will be born of a virgin	Isaiah 7:14	*"All this took place to fulfill what the Lord had spoken by the prophet: "Behold, the virgin shall conceive and bear a son, and they shall call his name Immanuel."*	Matthew 1:22–23; Luke 1:30–37
The Messiah will be the Wonderful Counselor, Mighty God, Everlasting Father, and Prince of Peace	Isaiah 9:6–7	*"For to us a child is born, unto us a son is given, and the government will be on his shoulders. And he will be called Wonderful Counselor, Mighty God, Everlasting Father, Prince of Peace."*	Luke 1:32–33; Matthew 12:42; Luke 1:32–33, 79; John 14:27; Acts 10:36; Romans 9:5; Colossians 2:3; 2 Thessalonians 3:3
The Messiah will be a King	Psalm 72; Isaiah 9:6-7; 32:1; Jeremiah 23:5; Zechariah 9:9; 14:9	Jesus will be from the lineage of King David but greater than him	Matthew 21:1-7; Matthew 22:41-45; Mark 12:35-37; Luke 20:41-44; Acts 2:34-36; 1 Corinthians 15:25-28; Hebrews 1:3, 13; 4:14–5:10
The Messiah is called the Son of Man	Genesis 3:15; 22:18; Isaiah 7:14-16; 9:6	Jesus came in the flesh as a man.	Matthew 1:18-21; John 1:14; Mark 8:31
The Messiah is called God	Isaiah 9:6; 40:3-5; 47:4; Jeremiah 23:5-6	Jesus named *Immanuel*, meaning *God with us.*	Matthew 1:23
The Messiah would be called God's son	Psalm 2:7	*"A voice came from heaven: 'You are my beloved Son; with you I am well pleased.'"*	Mark 1:11; Luke 3:22; Acts 4:25–28; Acts 13:33 Hebrews 1:5; 5:5

MESSIANIC PROPHECIES OF JESUS CHRIST			
Prophecy	Old Testament Scripture	Summary	New Testament Fulfillment
The Messiah will be the Light of the World	Isaiah 7:14; 9:1–2; 42:1-7	One who shines light; be a light for the nations.	Matthew 12:15–21; Luke 2:27–32; John 1:3-5, 3:16, 8:12, 9:5; Revelation 21:23–24
The Messiah will be a willing sacrifice	Genesis 22:1–18	*"For God so loved the world, that he gave his only Son, that whoever believes in him should not perish but have eternal life."*	John 3:16; Hebrews 11:17–19
The Messiah will be Passover Lamb	Exodus 12:3, 7–13	*"The next day he saw Jesus coming toward him, and said, "Behold, the Lamb of God, who takes away the sin of the world!"*	John 1:29; John 1:36, 19:33, 36; 1 Corinthians 5:7–8; 1 Peter 1:19
The Messiah will be the Star coming out of Jacob	Numbers 24:17	*"Now after Jesus was born in Bethlehem of Judea in the days of Herod the king, behold, wise men from the east came to Jerusalem, saying, "Where is he who has been born King of the Jews? For we saw his star when it rose and have come to worship him."*	Matthew 2:1–2; Revelation 22:16
The Messiah will be a prophet like Moses	Deuteronomy 18:15, 18–19	*"When the people saw the sign that he had done, they said, "This is indeed the Prophet who is to come into the world!""*	Matthew 13:57; 21:46; Luke 24:19; John 1:21, 25; 6:14; 7:40; Acts 3:22; 7:37
The Messiah will be forsaken and pierced, but vindicated	Psalm 22:1, 16–18	"So, they said to one another, "Let us not tear it, but cast lots for it to see whose it shall be." This was to fulfill the Scripture which says, "They divided my garments among them, and for my clothing they cast lots.""	Matthew 27:35, 39, 43–44, 46; Mark 15:34; John 19:23–24, 30; Hebrews 2:11–12
The Messiah will be resurrected	Psalm 16:8–11	*"For David, after he had served the purpose of God in his own generation, fell asleep and was laid with his fathers and saw corruption, but he whom God raised up did not see corruption."*	Acts 2:22–32, Acts 13:35–37

Jesus Christ's Conception and Birth

The story of the man Jesus Christ begins with His birth. Unlike any other, Jesus was born of a virgin woman but conceived by the Holy Spirit. Like us, He experienced all stages of growth into a man.

Jesus' Parents

His Mother, Mary

In the natural birth process, a woman named Mary delivered Jesus. Thus, He had a family lineage. Almighty God Himself conceived Jesus through the Holy Spirit. We believe that the one who declares Himself as the great "I AM," Almighty God, can easily pull off something like this.

God chose this virgin woman to carry and bring forth Jesus into the world. She had never had sexual relations with any man. This conception showed God's glory and Jesus' uniqueness. Some sects want to tie a divine element to Jesus' mother, Mary, but Scripture does not support this. Scripture reveals nothing divine about Mary except her virginity. When an angel told Mary about God's plan, she had to decide whether to accept it, just as the prophets and Christ's followers did. She does.

Mary humbly acknowledges her lowly estate to take part with God in something so important. In fact, in Mary's praise to God, she recognized this process as an unusual thing, debased herself to a servant, and acknowledged and gave God praise. Luke 1:46-55 records her song of praise. People consider her blessed to this day. However, again, there is nothing in Scripture that ascribes any divinity to Mary. She cannot and does not hear or answer prayers. She was an ordinary young woman whom God selected to be Jesus' mother. Who she was carrying inside her was divine.

What we *should* admire and seek to emulate about Mary is her self-abasement and willingness to take part with God in such an unorthodox plan. She told the angel, *I am the Lord's servant. May your word to me be fulfilled* (Luke 1:38 NIV). I'm sure this was frightening to Mary. She had never had a sexual relationship, yet God wanted to impregnate her. I'm sure it flashed through her mind what her family, religious community, and her fiancé might think.

Put yourself in her shoes. An angel appears with an unusual message: "You will conceive a child, never knowing a man...," "He will be great...," "He is the Messiah." Honestly, if it were me,

I'd be "shaking in my boots" at the appearance of an angel. I might run out of the room in a panic. And I'd be worried about my excellent reputation being tarnished. *"What will the church people think? My fiancé? We're planning a beautiful wedding; he won't want me anymore. Can you find someone else, God? I have too much to lose."* These are some thoughts we may have. Also consider the time in which Mary lived. Getting pregnant out of wedlock back then was unlike today. It was unacceptable and demanded death by stoning. Yikes!

But Mary willingly trusted God and agreed to take part in His plan. So, Jesus was miraculously conceived by the Holy Spirit but delivered through a woman's womb. Jesus Christ carried Mary's DNA.

(You can read this account in Luke 1:26-38.)

His Father, Joseph

Scripture does not provide much detail about Joseph, aside from what is key and what God wanted us to know. He revered God and was a righteous man who kept the law. Scripture reveals how Joseph raised Jesus as his natural-born son, although he was really His stepfather. (Any stepfathers reading this?)

Joseph and Mary were betrothed. Betrothal in Bible times was a binding legal agreement, making the couple husband and wife in God's eyes, even before a marriage ceremony today. (Think of being engaged in our time.)

Joseph learns Mary is pregnant. In those times, the woman would move into the husband's home, and the two would consummate the marriage by coming together sexually. When a man engaged a woman for marriage, they had to wait a year before coming together to ensure the woman had no other relations with a man. Not what is customary today, is it? Imagine how Mary felt knowing she had to tell Joseph she was pregnant. OMG!

No doubt this news devastated and confused him. *"How could she?"* he may have thought. He truly loved her, though, because he decided to put Mary away secretly to avoid her being shamed or killed. God intervenes, however. Another angel appears to tell Joseph he did not need to do this. He could safely take Mary as his wife. The angel explains to him that the Holy Spirit caused her to conceive. He need not fear embarrassment and scorn, or her demise. Joseph believed this message and took Mary as his wife but did not have sexual relations with her until after the baby was born. This is an astounding feat for Joseph to wait to have sexual relations with a wife who is now your own. What respect for God, what self-control, and selflessness.

Picture the stares and the difficulties Jesus' parents faced while trying to live everyday normal lives in their town. We all know about nosy neighbors; there's one in just about every neighborhood. They may have thought their story sounded like hogwash and spread this gossip. The women may have looked down on Mary, considering her a loose woman. You see, the Jewish religious culture follows the teachings in the Torah. They must follow the law. Although prophecies had circulated about a coming Messiah King through a virgin woman, many forgot and did not realize that this was it.

According to this account, Joseph's DNA does not reside in Jesus because he did not impregnate her; the Holy Spirit overshadowed Mary and impregnated her.

(You can read this account in Matthew 1:18-25.)

Jesus' Name

A baby's name is important. Sometimes, it comes to the parents while carrying the child. Some couples already have a name chosen for their child or have opted for a family member's name. As for Jesus' name, the prophecies spoken by the angel to both Mary and Joseph are consistent regarding what His name should be.

The angel told Mary in Luke 1:31-33 (NIV), *You will conceive and give birth to a son, and you are to call him Jesus. He will be great and will be called the Son of the Most High. The Lord God will give him the throne of his father David, and he will reign over Jacob's descendants forever; his kingdom will never end.*

To Joseph, the angel said in Matthew 1:20-21 (NIV), *But after he had considered this, an angel of the Lord appeared to him in a dream and said, Joseph son of David, do not be afraid to take Mary home as your wife, because what is conceived in her is from the Holy Spirit. She will give birth to a son, and you are to give him the name Jesus, because he will save his people from their sins.* Wow! Outstanding, right? No confusion or chaos; just a perfect plan unfolding. God guided them every step of the way through this extraordinary event.

In a December 2022 article called "With God, All Problems Eventually Fade," Pastor Chuck Swindoll notes how "God picked [the name] Jesus, a shorter version of Joshua, which means "SAVIOR." That Jesus came to save is the essence of His message. His first impression! The word of salvation is God's first word to us through the personal name of His Son. Christ's first step toward us is not as our Creator and King. It's as our loyal, merciful, fierce, loving *Savior*.... We need saving from many things—demons, depression, distress, deceit, death—but the angel specified *why* Joseph must name Him Jesus, 'for he will save his people from their sins'" (Matthew 1:21) (Swindoll).

This is the child Mary and Joseph had to raise into a man—Jesus, the Christ. What a responsibility!

Jesus' Birthday

We do not know the exact date Jesus Christ was born, but we celebrate His birth during the Christmas season. People debate how the date of December 25th came to be.

Nonetheless, Jesus was born. Luke 2:1-7 (NIV) records, *In those days Caesar Augustus issued a decree that a census should be taken of the entire Roman world. (This was the first census that took place while Quirinius was governor of Syria.) And everyone went to their own town to register. So, Joseph also went up from the town of Nazareth in Galilee to Judea, to Bethlehem, the town of David, because he belonged to the house and line of David. He went there to register with Mary, who was pledged to be his wife and was expecting a child. While they were there, the time came for the baby to be born, and she gave birth to her firstborn, a son. She wrapped him in cloths and placed him in a manger, because there was no guest room available for them.*

Nearby, outside the town, Luke 2:8-14 (NIV) tells us, *And there were shepherds living out in the fields nearby, keeping watch over their flocks at night. An angel of the Lord appeared to them, and the glory of the Lord shone around them, and they were terrified. But the angel says to them, 'Do not be afraid. I bring you good news that will cause great joy for all the people. Today in the town of David, a Savior has been born to you; he is the Messiah, the Lord. This will be a sign to you: You will find a baby wrapped in cloths and lying in a manger.' Suddenly, a great company of the heavenly host appeared with the angel, praising God and saying, 'Glory to God in the highest heaven, and on earth peace to those on whom his favor rests.* (Do you notice how the angels are busy on assignment for God in this situation, and have the *same* message?)

These were challenging times in which Christ was born. Political unrest, social upheaval, and oppression gripped the area, like today. Filled with jealousy and consternation over someone taking his place, the ruling king received words about the birth of a king. He asked traveling wise men about the location of this birth. The wise men recognized Jesus' birth because they saw a star in the sky that signaled this event. They followed this star, found Jesus, worshiped Him, and brought Him unique gifts. They knew He was the promised Messiah King. So, they did not report Jesus' location to the ruling king because they knew he meant to harm H. The king had ordered the death of all newborn children ages two and under. Joseph received a warning about this plot in a dream, so he and Mary escaped to Egypt to protect Jesus' life. Finally, the ruling king died, and Joseph received the all-clear that it was now safe to return to Israel with the child. They returned and lived in Nazareth.

(You can read this account in Matthew 2:1-23.)

Jesus' Race and Culture

Jesus was born Jewish in Bethlehem. He had a familial lineage that practiced and followed Judaism (Luke 3:31 and John 4:9). This is important because there is no way Jesus could fully identify with us unless He experienced the whole gamut of familial, cultural, and religious experiences as we do. People subjected the Jews to oppression and political control.

Jesus' Siblings and Upbringing

Matthew 13:55 tells us that Joseph worked as a carpenter to support his wife and family. Jesus was the eldest child, but his parents had more children. Mark 6:3 (also in Matthew) tells us Jesus had four younger brothers and at least two sisters. The passage doesn't include the sisters' names, but it lists the names of His brothers: James (in Hebrew, Jacob), Joses (in Hebrew, Joseph, after his father), Simon, and Judas (also known as Jude).

As was customary, Jesus and His brothers likely learned the carpenter's trade from their father and may have traveled throughout the town, building and repairing homes and temples. Thus, Jesus can identify with work and holding down a job. His father died, and His mother was alone. I'm sure He cared for her in His earthly father's absence.

Little documentation exists about Jesus' younger life, except for the account when He was twelve years old. Joseph and Mary traveled to Jerusalem each year for the Passover Feast. One year, they realized Jesus was missing, and they searched for Him for three days. They found Him in the temple courts, where He was talking with and asking questions of the elders and teachers, who were amazed by His understanding at such a young age. Jesus was already garnering attention at such an early age. I'm sure it was difficult to raise such a peculiar child, who was the Messiah Christ. **(See Luke 2:41-52.)**

You can find out more about Jesus' younger years in Luke 2:39-40 (NIV). There's not much, but it says, *When Joseph and Mary had done everything required by the Law of the Lord, they returned to Galilee to their own town of Nazareth. And the child grew and became strong; he was filled with wisdom, and the grace of God was on him.* And Luke 2:52 (ESV) states, *"And Jesus increased in wisdom and in stature and in favor with God and man."* As we have grown up, Jesus, too, matured physically, developmentally, and socially. So, Jesus was a Gen Alpha! 😊

Since this is all Scripture records about Jesus' younger years, we can only imagine what He was like. We can draw conclusions based on the Jewish customs Jesus grew up under, as well as the typical nature and attributes of young children. However, we cannot accept or make any emphatic statements about Jesus' younger life. We can only infer from these writings that Jesus was wise beyond his years, grew up, had a rapport with people, and once put his parents in a quandary (like our kids do) when He wandered away from them. LOL.

Jesus shared our human experience, including being of a specific race, growing up in a cultural context, practicing a religion's traditions, and possibly experiencing sibling rivalry.

A Significant Cousin

Notice how strategic God is in this next section regarding extended family relationships. Concurrently, Mary conceived Jesus, and her cousin Elizabeth, who was old, also became pregnant. Elizabeth gave birth to John, who was Jesus' cousin. We know him as John the Baptist, and he was significant to Jesus' ministry. Mary visited her relative, and from the womb the babies recognized one another; John leaped in Elizabeth's womb upon hearing Mary's greeting. **(See Luke 1:1-25, Luke 1:57-66.)**

John the Baptist was the forerunner to Jesus' ministry, announcing the Messiah's coming and building followers whom he baptized. John did not think himself worthy to baptize Jesus but did so before Jesus began His public ministry (John 1:26-27). He was making disciples and proclaiming the Kingdom of God but never equated himself with Jesus Christ. In fact, he humbled himself and told the crowds he was not the one prophesied about. He explained that another was coming who was greater than himself. John knew his place compared to his cousin. He was okay with staying in his lane. Are you in your lane or someone else's? Is the Christian leadership at your church making it clear that they are not the great ones? Or do you find yourself often resorting to, "My bishop or pastor said..." or "The covenant rules state we should..." OMG!

It's important to note here how Jesus' cousin put Jesus on "blast" (in a good way). I understand the term is used on social media in a negative context to expose, embarrass, or hold someone accountable. I'm not using it that way. John openly proclaimed Jesus as the Messiah and baptized people to prepare them for Christ's message. He blasted Jesus so much that when Jesus began His ministry, crowds knew He was the Messiah. John was not jealous or insecure. He had Jesus' back and prepared the way for Him to flow in His ministry.

Some of Jesus' family cooperated with God and His plan for sending Jesus. This could have inconvenienced them and troubled their lives because they lived in a community that followed stringent laws and, in the past, had unfairly treated them. Some did not believe in or follow Him during His earthly ministry, but they did after His death and resurrection. So, if your family you've been praying for years still does not believe and has not yet accepted Jesus Christ, don't despair, don't give up. Jesus also experienced disbelief from within His family, but He kept going.

So, Jesus can relate to having extended family relationships. Possibly, He attended family reunions and gatherings. While they did not have elaborate Bar and Bat Mitzvah ceremonies in His time, I'm sure He would have gone to support His friends. He also understands how family members can play a significant part in your ministry.

(See Matthew 3:1-12, 4:12—17; Mark 1:1-8, 14-15; Luke 3:1-20; John 1:19-39; John 3:22-36.)

Conclusion

Of course, many people have disputed or challenged these facts about Jesus over the centuries, and they continue to do so today. As Walter Elwell writes, "Everyone approaches sources from a point of view that either includes, excludes, or leaves open the possibility of what is recorded. Given Christian presuppositions, the story makes perfect sense; given non-Christian presuppositions, the rejection of the sources as unreliable is understandable. It is not really a question of the sources, but a question of the interpreter of the sources" (Elwell).

Followers of Jesus Christ believe these facts. We recognize the incomprehensible plan

God put in place before Jesus appeared, at His conception and birth, and into His adulthood when He began His public ministry. He put together everything that needed to be accomplished for His Son, Jesus Christ, to enter the world. Although Jesus was born in an obscure place, He was well-raised with a father and mother, had siblings, and extended family relationships. So, He knows about this family paradigm and can relate to us.

The crucial points to keep in mind here are the extraordinary, unconventional methods God used and the supernatural way in which Jesus Christ came to us. It was not typical, much like the way we see how God worked in times past with the Israelites. How have we become so typical in how we operate as Christians? Why have we confined God to such orthodoxy? Why are local churches copycats of each other? OMG!

Also significant to note is God's use of ordinary people in His plan. The Bible's characters are everyday people like us, leading normal lives until God intervenes, reveals His purpose, and asks them to join in. Most times, it goes beyond what we would think or imagine or is something that exceeds our ability to accomplish.

Jesus Christ's story of His conception and birth defies scientific explanation. It's inconceivable to the natural mind. Throughout history, there are no stories of another human being conceived *without* sexual relations or artificial insemination, where the male's sperm is required. This is the crux of Jesus' uniqueness. While Jesus Christ came as a man and shared all the natural, earthly elements as us, the unique aspect about Him was *who He came from* and *by what means*. That's the difference. OMG!

In your own time, read these accounts. No matter your beliefs, whether Jewish, Roman, Greek, or otherwise, the Bible writers told us that the Old Testament foretold Jesus Christ, and the New Testament confirms Him.

Surely, He is an extraordinary Son of Man!

Chapter 6 - So, What Exactly Did Jesus Do?

We've discovered how Jesus came to earth and lived as a man just as you and I. He was young and likely went to school, and his father trained him in a building trade. He experienced family life with his parents and siblings, who taught and raised him in the Jewish religion. All that we experience. But, as he matured into his 30s, the time came for Him to fulfill His life's mission. He had to implement the things for which God sent Him to the earth. What was that? What did Jesus do when He approached His millennial years?

Another prophecy about Jesus Christ, the Messiah, is in the Old Testament book of Isaiah, chapter 61 (NIV). It tells us Jesus would do life-affirming, redemptive deeds. It states about Jesus,

The Spirit of the Sovereign Lord is on me,
because the Lord has anointed me
to proclaim good news to the poor.
He has sent me to bind up the brokenhearted,
to proclaim freedom for the captives,
and release from darkness for the prisoners.
To proclaim the year of the Lord's favor...
instead of a spirit of despair...

When you have a chance, read the entire chapter. It's interesting. Once, while standing to read this verse of scripture to the congregation in the synagogue, Jesus said to them, *Today this scripture is fulfilled in your hearing.* (Luke 4:16-21 NIV).

Also, one of the biblical authors writes in the New Testament book of Acts 10:38 (ESV) ... *how God anointed Jesus of Nazareth with the Holy Spirit and with power. He went about doing good and healing all who were oppressed by the devil, for God was with him.*

A few keywords about Jesus merit attention:

- He **was anointed**.
- He **had the Holy Spirit and power**.
- He **spoke goodness, not despair.**
- He **did good**.
- **God was with Him**.

Isaiah 61 tells us what Christ would do on earth. You'll see. Jesus' statement to the congregants that the verse was fulfilled in their presence meant He was the One, and He would prove it through His actions. Both verses emphasize how Jesus was anointed to be and do all He did. Also, the scripture in Acts, which was written after Jesus left the earth, confirms that Jesus did what Isaiah 61 prophesied.

Therefore, Jesus Christ's life and actions serve as obvious examples for Christians and His followers to emulate. His character and conduct were exemplary, offering a model of goodness for all to follow.

How Jesus Christ Did What He Did

In addition, recall the angelic messages proclaimed about Jesus to His parents, the shepherds, and the prophets, which said:

- He **is the Son of God**.
- He **is from the Holy Spirit**.
- He **will save people from sin**.
- He **will proclaim good news, not bad — that will bring great joy** to all the people.
- He **would be great and rule and reign** over a never-ending kingdom.

These proclamations align with the prophecy in Isaiah 61 and underscore the importance of discerning Jesus' true purpose, particularly given the frequent misuse of His name today. Jesus Christ came to reveal what God and His kingdom are like. His message and actions were entirely new; people, even in their religious community, had never heard such things. The community thought they knew God's ways, but when Jesus spoke and acted, they realized they did not. Likewise, when Christ first saves us, the experience is new. We know little about life in Christ or what it means to be a Christian. That's why reading the Bible and attending church matter. New life in Christ is a journey that takes a lifetime, one that you will never master in this life.

In everything Jesus said and did in His teachings, actions, and interactions, He was revealing God and how humanity could relate with Him. This was His primary purpose.

We know this is so because you will notice in scripture how Jesus often said that He was not speaking for or of Himself. He often said that His works were not coming from Himself, but from the Father, God. He was receiving instructions from God. He *always* said and did things that pleased the Father, God, and He had to humble Himself and submit to God to do so (John 8:29). I tell you this because we should think of Jesus Christ as our prototype if we are truly following Him, bringing God glory, and making Him known to the world. Jesus is the model or example of what God intends for humanity. He is the ultimate expression of God's character and the standard for how we should live as Christians.

Unfortunately, this is not the belief of some Christians today. People have misconstrued the term "Christian," and they have adopted many erroneous ideals about its meaning. Jesus Christ is the leader of the Christian faith. We don't set the precedent for what a Christian is or what a Christian does. Jesus did. He is the way into the Christian faith (not the Christian religion). Christianity is not a religion; it's a life of faith in and identity with and allegiance to Jesus Christ. Historically, followers of Jesus were first called "Christians" in the city of Antioch. Acts 11:25-26 (NIV) tells us this. It says, *Then Barnabas went to Tarsus to look for Saul, and when he found him, he brought him to Antioch. So for a whole year, Barnabas and Saul met with the church and taught great numbers of people. The disciples were called Christians first at Antioch.* May I ask if you knew this? In Antioch, they were meeting together, teaching about Jesus, and Gentile nonbelievers were being accepted and now coming to Christ. The early church was redefined when they identified as "Christians," separating them from other Jewish groups and proving that the Gospel's message was for everyone. The city of Antioch was very diverse, showing the Gospel's goal of including everyone. OMG!

What it Means to be Anointed

We generally attribute this term to specific ministers or individuals who perform acts or work in God's kingdom. We consider someone to be anointed based on how eloquently or forcefully they speak, preach, or teach, or how well they sing. This is especially true in the Pentecostal, COGIC, or faith word movement. It's based on how these people stir us. "Boy, didn't the pastor preach today?" we say. Someone's being anointed has nothing to do with how well they stir our emotions.

For Jesus, His name with the title "the Christ" means the Anointed One. Messiah also means "one who has been anointed." The verse says about Jesus, "*because the Lord has anointed Him...*" That's humongous and important for followers of Jesus Christ to know. As His followers, who would do the same or greater works than He did, we too need God's anointing. So, what then does it mean for God's people to be anointed? In Hebrew, "anointed" simply means someone who is designated to carry out an assigned task. Therefore, we are anointed simply when we fulfill the calling God gives us.

The Bible Project produced an excellent video that explains the word "anointing" in easy language. You can watch this video at https://bibleproject.com/explore/video/anointing/.

Jesus' anointed life and ministry among the people He encountered or spent time with brought about a change in them. Even when people opposed and challenged Him, Jesus was anointed to stand up against them and declare His truth. Later, many people became silent or were convicted. We rarely think about needing an anointing to argue for truth. God assigned Jesus Christ to do all the works He did for and among the people. He anointed him. Therefore, it's essential that we understand the task for which the Lord has anointed us; it's there that we will have the greatest impact.

What Jesus Christ Did

The Consummate Minister

Jesus was an astounding preacher and consummate teacher. Most of us don't distinguish between the two, but there's a difference. Founder of Ligonier Ministries, Dr. R.C. Sproul notes, "Typically, we distinguish between preaching and teaching. Preaching involves activities such as exhortation, exposition, admonition, encouragement, and comfort, while teaching involves the transfer of information and instruction in various subject areas. However, there is much overlap between the two. Preaching must communicate content and include teaching, and teaching people the things of God cannot be done neutrally but must exhort them to heed and obey the Word of Christ," (Sproul, Preaching and Teaching).

The most common word for a preacher in the New Testament was "herald," which explains what preaching meant. A herald was one who announced a message from the king or some other ruling authority to those who had not heard it before. Preaching in New Testament times, therefore, relates to announcing good news.

So then, as a preacher, Jesus proclaimed that the Kingdom of God had arrived. Luke 4:43 (NIV) confirms this. It says, *But he says, I must proclaim the good news of the kingdom of God to the other towns also, because that is why I was sent. And he kept on preaching in the synagogues of Judea.*

Scripture also says that after they imprisoned John the Baptist, Jesus moved to Capernaum and began preaching in Galilee. (See Matthew 4:12-17; Mark 1:14-15; Luke 4:14-15.) *From that time on, Jesus began to preach, 'Repent, for the kingdom of heaven has come near'* (Matthew 4:17 NIV). And Mark 1:38 (NIV) says, *Jesus replied, Let us go somewhere else—to the nearby villages—so I can preach there also. That is why I have come.*

So, we see, Jesus understood His calling and mission to preach or proclaim God's kingdom message, and He stayed in that lane and never deviated from it. Jesus preached in His hometown, other villages, on mountaintops, in the temple and synagogues, and on the streets.

A Unique Teacher

Jesus was also a profound teacher. He astounded the crowds in how he explained ideas, clarified controversial issues, settled debates, and exhorted people on how to live out God's kingdom life. He clarified God's perspective on things and how His kingdom thinks and operates; it's nothing like the way earthly kingdoms do. Benjamin L. Merkle writes an essay on The Gospel Coalition (TGC) U.S. Edition's website, *The Teachings of Jesus.* He states, "Jesus was the consummate teacher, not only because of how he taught, but because of what he taught. The following section will explain three prominent topics in Jesus' teachings: (1) the reality of the kingdom of God, (2) living in the kingdom of God, and (3) the Lord of the kingdom of God .... Jesus was known for his ability to teach. He is called 'teacher' forty-five times in the New Testament. The Aramaic title 'Rabbi' is used fourteen times of Jesus, even though he was not formally trained as a Rabbi" (Merkle). Rabbi is the official term for a teacher in the Jewish culture.

Jesus Christ taught from boats, by the sea, in people's homes, in the desert, wherever He could. He often isolated himself from the crowds to pray and get the mind of God. (See Mark 1:35, Matthew 14:23, Luke 6:12, and John 6:15.) He always needed to gain God's perspective for where to go and what to say and do. So should we. We cannot do God's will without talking to Him about it.

As a preacher and teacher, then, Jesus shared His wisdom and knowledge of Scripture in unusual ways. Full of goodness, Jesus showed love by meeting people's needs and performing good deeds for them. Jesus had authority and power, and He performed supernatural miracles and healings that defied science. As the leader, He selected, taught, and sent out His disciples to do the same things. And they did.

The Works of Jesus Christ

See the infographics, which feature some of Jesus' sermons, teachings, miracles, and healings He performed. These will give you an idea of what Jesus Christ was really all about.

SERMONS JESUS PREACHED

1. **Five Discourses of Matthew refer to five specific discourses by Jesus within the Gospel of Matthew. Discourses are simply extended sermons, teachings, or conversations that Jesus spoke to people.**

   a. **The Sermon on the Mount is one of Jesus' most notable sermons.** Read it in Matthew 5-7. Here, He gives the Beatitudes, which are a set of eight blessings given by Jesus. The term "Beatitudes" comes from the Latin word "beatus" or beatitude," meaning blessed or happy. It's a collection of teachings on various aspects of Christian living. Also, He describes the characteristics and attitudes of those who are truly blessed in God's eyes; they are promised rewards in the Kingdom of Heaven. You may recognize one beatitude, which says, *Blessed are the merciful, for they shall obtain mercy.*

   b. **The Missionary Discourse - Matthew 10:1-42.** Here, Jesus commissions his twelve apostles on a mission to preach the Gospel and heal the sick, with specific instructions for their travel, emphasizing to "keep it simple" and to rely on God to provide. They are to preach to the lost sheep of Israel, heal, cast out demons, and warn of persecution and division. Jesus assures them they will be given the words to speak when needed.

   c. **The Parabolic of the Discourse in Matthew 13** presents a series of parables concerning the Kingdom of Heaven. These parables are Jesus' way of teaching about God's kingdom to his disciples and are often interpreted as revealing the nature and growth of the Kingdom of Heaven.

   d. **The Discourse on the Church in Matthew 18** is also known as the Ecclesial Discourse. This sermon outlines the principles for the establishment and life of the church, emphasizing humility, forgiveness, and the importance of the apostles' leadership. It also connects this earthly church to the future Kingdom of Heaven and the final judgment.

   e. **The Olivet Discourse - Matthew 24 and 25.** Jesus addresses his disciples on the Mount of Olives on various end-time topics, including the destruction of the Jerusalem temple, the signs of the end times, and the Second Coming of Christ.

2. **Jesus' Proclamation of a New Kingdom -** The kingdom of God is a spiritual reality and a future, literal kingdom He rules. A new way of life characterizes it. Christ said the kingdom He was from and ruled was not of this world (John 18:36). Many of Jesus' sermons then contrasted what was being taught or done during the time and within the culture He lived. What is the kingdom like? (Luke 13:18-21). Tells the Pharisees that the Kingdom of God has no observable signs but is in their midst, alluding to Himself (Luke 17:20-21).

3. **Bread of Life Discourse – (John 6:22-59)** It highlights Jesus as the source of true spiritual sustenance and eternal life.

4. **Jesus' Farewell Discourse – (John 13-17 and Matthew 23:1-39)** This is Jesus' last sermon to His disciples before His crucifixion. It emphasizes love, unity, and the coming of the Holy Spirit. Jesus washes the disciples' feet, promises them help, and prays for them during this long discourse.

Jesus' Teachings

Scripture tells us in Luke 21:37-38 (NIV), *"Each day Jesus was teaching at the temple, and each evening he went out to spend the night on the hill called the Mount of Olives. And all the people came early in the morning to hear him at the temple."* Every day? Wow! That's a lot. Most church congregations today hold Bible studies once a week.

Jesus makes it clear in John 7:14-18 (NIV) what He was teaching. Questions arose about His knowledge of scripture with no formal training. It reads, *Not until halfway through the festival did Jesus go up to the temple courts and begin to teach. The Jews there were amazed and asked, 'How did this man get such learning without having been taught?' Jesus answered, My teaching is not my own. It comes from the one who sent me. Anyone who chooses to do the will of God will find out whether my teaching comes from God or whether I speak on my own. Whoever speaks on their own does so to gain personal glory, but he who seeks the glory of the one who sent him is a man of truth; there is nothing false about him.*

Are you now able to recognize what I was telling you earlier — how Jesus always proclaimed that what He was doing and saying came from God? We must examine whether our teaching originates from God's heart, or our own intellect, a synopsis of a problem, current affairs, or our worldview. Are we seeking glory (magnificence, radiance, power, beauty) for ourselves?

Let's examine a few notable teachings of Jesus that can guide us during these challenging times in our world.

TEACHINGS OF JESUS	RELATING SCRIPTURES
Jesus' teaching on prayer ("Our Father, who art in heaven...")	Matthew 6:5-15; Luke 11:1-13
Jesus' teaching about **worry**	Matthew 6:25-34
Jesus' teaching on **loving our enemies (The Sermon on the Plain)**	Luke 6:27-36
Jesus' teaching on **fearing God, not people**	Matthew 10:26-32
Jesus' teaching about **our burdens, weariness, and stress**	Matthew 11:28-30
Jesus' teaching on **what it means to follow Him**	Mark 8:34-38
Jesus' teaching on **hearing and doing the word**	Matthew 7:24-27
Jesus' teaching **about the vine and branches; remaining in Him**	John 15:1-17
Jesus' teaching about **what greatness really looks like in God's kingdom**	Matthew 20:20-28. Mark 10:35-45
Jesus' teaching **against anger and murder**	Matthew 5:21-26
Jesus' teaching about **adultery and divorce**	Matthew 5:28 and 19:1-11
Jesus' teaching of **where true defilement comes from**	Matthew 15:10-20
Jesus' teaching **about little children**	Matthew 19:13-15
Jesus' teaching **about the greatest commandment**	Matthew 22:34-40
Jesus' interesting statement about a **lack of faith, respect from one's race of origin, family, culture, and community**	Mark 6:4-6 and Matthew 13:57-58

How Jesus Christ Taught

Benjamin Merkle also tells us how, "Jesus used a variety of teaching techniques to impress his teaching on his hearers. Such techniques were used to clarify his meaning, motivate (or sometimes shock) the listeners, or reveal the true intent of God's Word—all the while making his teaching memorable. Some forms of Jesus' teaching include poetry, proverbs, exaggeration, and parables, and many others (such as puns (Matt. 23:24), similes (Luke 17:6), metaphors (Matt. 5:13-14), riddles (Mark 14:58), paradoxes (Mark 12:41-44), irony (Matt. 16:2-3), and questions (Mark 3:1-4)" (Merkle).

Jesus was known to teach in parables. It's how he drove home a lesson he was teaching or illustrated a more profound and valuable moral lesson. A parable uses the whole story to teach a lesson, unlike a proverb, metaphor, simile, or figure of speech, which focus on a word, phrase, or sentence. The parables of Jesus make up a crucial part of the Bible. Jesus had the wisdom to convey profound spiritual truths to humanity in relatable stories that were uncomplicated. The source definition of the word "parable" means a comparison placed side by side. Sometimes, the Gospel authors begin a parable with an analogy, such as The Parable of the Sower, which teaches us about receiving the Word of God (Google A.I.)

PARABLES OF JESUS		
PARABLES	**SUMMARY**	**RELATING SCRIPTURES**
Parable of the Sower	Jesus uses a story about a farmer who scatters seed to illustrate different ways people respond to the message of the kingdom of heaven. It emphasizes the importance of receiving God's word with a receptive heart and how varied factors can hinder its growth and fruitfulness.	Matthew 13:1-23
Parable of the Good Samaritan	Jesus' telling of this parable is to show how loving one's neighbor is to care about/for their needs and help them.	Luke 10:25-37
Parable of the Rich Landowner	Tells the story of how wealth and amassing possessions as one's primary focus in life is not wise, as these can produce greed and do not ensure long life or security. True richness lies in being "rich toward God".	Luke 12:13-21
Parable where Jesus proclaims the superiority of the new over the old. New Wine in New Wineskins	Parable of the New Garment and Patch. Jesus explains that tearing a piece from a new garment to patch an old one would ruin both, just as the new teachings of Jesus would not fit within the old ways. The old is preferable: Jesus concludes by saying that no one who has drunk old wine wants new wine, as they prefer the familiar and established. This suggests that the established religious traditions would be resistant to the new message He brings.	Matthew 9:14-17; Mark 2:18-22; Luke 5:33-39
Parable of the Lost Sheep and Coin	In these parables, Jesus illustrates God's boundless love and concern for sinners and the immense value God places on individuals, even those who seem insignificant.	Luke 15:3-7 and 15:8-10
Parable of the Compassionate Father	Also known as the Parable of the Prodigal Son, it is a story about a man with two sons. The younger son receives his inheritance and wastes it, but he eventually returns home and is welcomed back with open arms. The parable highlights God's unwavering love and forgiveness, even for those who have strayed far from Him.	(Luke 15:11-32).
Parable of the Unforgiving Slave	This illustrates the importance of extending mercy and forgiveness to others, just as God has shown us mercy and forgiveness.	Matthew 18:23-35
Parable of the Mustard Seed	This illustrates the idea that God's kingdom, though seemingly small at its beginnings, will grow into something very large and influential.	Matthew 13:31-32

Where Jesus Preached and Taught

- Jesus taught in the temple (for us today, this could be in church). Luke 21:37-38 (NIV) tells us, *Each day Jesus was teaching at the temple, and each evening he went out to spend the night on the hill called the Mount of Olives, and all the people came early in the morning to hear him at the temple.* We know Jesus had a fascination with the Temple because, remember, at twelve years old, it's where his mother and father found him conversing with the religious leaders, and they were amazed at Jesus' understanding, wisdom, and insight.
- Jesus taught one-on-one (John 3:1-21).
- Jesus taught small groups (Matthew 11:1).
- Jesus taught large crowds on mountainsides, by the sea, or from boats (Matthew 5:1-2; Mark 3:7-12).

As you read for yourself, notice how Jesus' teaching and preaching amazed and astounded people; they had never heard such teachings or experienced such authority in the way He taught. He taught with authority, surpassing even the experts in the law, because God was with Him and He had the power of the Holy Spirit working through His messages. His teachings were powerful and true (Mark 1:21-28). His teachings also angered the religious establishment and caused him trouble. Are your preaching and teaching raising eyebrows?

To Whom Did Jesus Preach and Teach

Traveling from town to town by boat, Jesus taught in His own neighborhood and the surrounding villages to whoever would listen. Scripture is clear that sizable crowds followed Jesus to hear Him, so that would include anyone. And Jesus was developing a greater rapport with the people and drawing thousands.

He also spent extra time teaching and training His committed group of twelve followers, explaining His words to them (Matthew 7:28-29). He later commissions, anoints, equips, and sends them out, and they were not perfect. It's also interesting to note that Jesus took the twelve disciples with Him on His preaching expeditions.

Jesus Christ's Demonstrations of Goodness and Power

The New Testament biblical writers tell us how Jesus went around doing good for others. As a holy man, we learn in Acts 10:38 (NIV), where it says about Jesus, *...how God anointed Jesus of Nazareth with the Holy Spirit and power, and how He went around doing good and healing all who were under the power of the devil, because God was with Him.* Doesn't this verse complement the prophecies we just read?

You may wonder what precisely, then, was this good Jesus did for others? And how did He do it? Because He was truly "all good" and wanted to please the Father, God, He had pure intentions and wanted nothing in return. *None of what He did involved any money.* "God gave His only Son," remember? For sure, Jesus was extraordinary. He had a special anointing by God's Holy Spirit, the scripture verse says, and He relied on and drew from the Holy Spirit's power to be and do all the good He did. This is how He could accomplish His work and complete His mission.

Jesus' works were not the work of the devil or performed by magic, as some in Scripture assert they were. Because Jesus came down from God the Father, He had so much power, spiritual gifts, and abilities, which He used to fulfill His purpose.

Jesus' public ministry is the period during which Jesus began fulfilling His purpose of serving others. It's when He gathered a team and began interacting with the people in His region, teaching, preaching, healing, and showing God's works. Matthew 4:23-25 illustrates this.

Jesus was in His early thirties (a Millennial 😊) when He began His public ministry. for only three and a half years, but in such a brief period, He changed the world and the course of history as no one ever has or will.

JESUS' DEMONSTRATIONS OF GOODNESS		
Demonstrated What God is Like	"Emmanuel, God with us."	Isaiah 7:14; Matthew 1:23
The Importance of Prayer	Time alone talking with God, the Father. He shows what our mindset should and should not be like when we pray. Jesus prays for the Father to glorify Him. Jesus prays for His disciples, believers everywhere, and believers to come (us).	Matthew 6:5-15; Luke 11:1-13 John 17:1-5; John 17:6-19; John 17:20-26
Demonstrated Servanthood	By washing the disciples' feet.	John 13:1-17
Demonstrated Love, Compassion, Mercy, Sympathy/Empathy,		
• **Showed Emotion**	He wept at the death of Lazarus and weeps for Jerusalem	John 11:1-5 Luke 19:41-44
• **Forgiveness**	Matthew 9:1-8; Mark 2:1-12; Luke 5:17-26	
• **Mercy**	John 8:1-11	
• **Inclusiveness/non-bias, Discrimination**	John 4:4-30, 39-42; Mark 7:24-30	
• **Feeds thousands**	Matthew 15:32-38; Mark 8:1-19	
• **Comforts people**	John 16:33; Matthew 11:28-30; Luke 23:43	
• **Fighting against temptation**	Matthew 4:1-11; Mark 1:12-13; Luke 4:1-13	

Demonstrated Authority Over the Physical and Demon World	Heals a boy with an unclean spirit. Heals a Gadarene, and the demons run into the pigs. Heals a demon-possessed blind and mute man. Rebuked demons and spirits and commanded them.	Luke 9:37-43 Matthew 8:28-34; Mark 5:1-20; Luke 8:26-39 Matthew 12:22 Luke 4:41
Demonstrated God's Power by Performing Miracles		

MIRACLES JESUS CHRIST PERFORMED	
Walks on water	Matthew 14:22-33
Raising the dead	John 11:8-44; Luke 7:11-15; Mark 5:21-24, 35-43
Calms storms	Mark 4:35-41
Feeds 4,000 with a little food	Matthew 15:29-39
Turns water into wine	John 2:1-11
Jesus' transformation before three disciples	Luke 9:28-36

HEALINGS JESUS PERFORMED		
Cleansing a leper	In Jesus' day, leprosy was associated with uncleanness, sin, and divine punishment. Jesus healed quite a few people with leprosy.	Matthew 8:1-4; Luke 17:11-19
Healing a centurion's servant	This was a Roman official.	Matthew 8:5-13
Raising a widow's son	There is hope for mothers.	Luke 7:11-17
Healing His disciple Peter's mother-in-law and many sick and demon-possessed	This was one of Jesus' own followers who was experiencing trouble.	Matthew 8:14-17
Healing and forgiving paralytics	Do you have a disability? I do (MS). The Lord has not yet healed me, but I believe.	Matthew 9:1-8; John 5:1-15
A woman with an issue of blood	This woman suffered for a long time, even after seeing many doctors.	Mark 5:25-34
Healing on the Sabbath	Jesus' healing works on the Sabbath offended the Jewish religious leaders.	Luke 14:1-6
Healing a royal official's son	Even those of a high-class status, Jesus healed.	John 4:46-54
Healing a deaf mute	Have a speech impediment?	Mark 7:31-37
Healed many others who were lame, blind crippled, mute, and more	The Lord can heal birth defects or defects that come at any age—autism spectrum disorder, retardation, spinal bifida, atrial septal defects, limb malformations, cleft lip and palate, microcephaly, down syndrome, sickle cell anemia, cystic fibrosis, deafness, cerebral palsy, and others. He can! What is most interesting about this story in John 9, Jesus' disciples asked, "Who sinned, him or his parents?" Jesus' reply, "Neither."	Matthew 15:29-31; Matthew 9:27-30; Matthew 9:28-31; John 9

HEALINGS JESUS PERFORMED		
Healing the blind	What I find very interesting in the John 9 story is when His disciples ask, "Who sinned, him or his parents? Jesus' replied, "Neither." The Lord can heal those born with birth defects – (autism spectrum disorder, intellectual disability, spina bifida, atrial septal defects, limb malformations, cleft lip and palate, microcephaly, Down syndrome, sickle cell anemia, cystic fibrosis, deafness, cerebral palsy, and others.	Matthew 9:27-31; Mark 8:22-25; John 9:1-11
Healing a withered hand	Have some of your body parts lost normal function? Mine have. Jesus can heal.	Matthew 12:9-14; Mark 3:1-6; Luke 6:6-11
Healing on the Sabbath-	Jesus' healing works on the Sabbath offended the Jewish religious leaders.	Luke 14:1-6
Healing a royal official's son	Jesus even healed those of an upper-class status.	John 4:46-54
Healing a deaf-mute	Have speech impediment? Jesusa can heal that!	Mark 7:31-37
Healed many others who were lame, blind, crippled, mute, and more		Matthew 15:29-31

So, my friends, it's clear from the Bible what Jesus Christ was all about, as revealed by what He said and did while on earth. It is also clear in the Bible what *those good things were*. Contrary to what is sometimes said about Him, He was more than just a good man; He was an outstanding teacher and rabbi. Jesus Christ, the Son of God, had authority from God and tremendous power to fulfill a specific mission. In all that Jesus was and did, and in how He interacted with the people of His time, He revealed God, pointed people to Him, and showed them how to treat fellow believers. This is crucial for us to know, believe, and study if we aim to keep Jesus Christ first in our lives and in the Church. This is what the disciples, apostles, and other biblical authors wrote about Jesus Christ.

Jesus has continued to be present for centuries since He left the earth, and the Church was started shortly after. Since Jesus' departure, people have misconstrued Christ's person, purpose, and mission. In fact, in each period, many ideas about Jesus Christ, the Bible, or Christianity were discussed and/or disputed by the people of that time. You can read about the debates that ensued in each era. Some have challenged these incorrect ideas because they have filtered into the thinking and practices of the Church. It's imperative as followers of Jesus Christ to correct erroneous information and stand for the truth.

As believers, we should try to emulate the early church's approach to church, which centered on exalting Jesus Christ's name and doing the works He did. This will involve our debasing ourselves so that God may be glorified. Wanting to become popular, or being self-focused, or attaining a high status or exalted position in the Church was not Christ's idea? The book of Acts shows how the Holy Spirit was present to support the early Church. OMG!

It was during the Enlightenment era, spanning from the mid-17th century to the late 18th century, that the greatest philosophers and intellectual minds studied the Bible while applying their philosophical viewpoints. Deism was a widely accepted view then. Deists believe people can know God by using their minds and looking at nature, not by listening to prophets or believing in religious messages. These thinkers rejected the possibility of miracles and other supernatural events described in the Bible. They held that there is a God, but He does not intervene in the universe. They challenged traditional authority and believed that humanity could improve through rational change. Many saw Jesus as a great moral teacher rather than a divine figure. One of the U.S. presidents even omitted all supernatural claims of Jesus' miracles and his resurrection. They believe that the New Testament Gospels are not eyewitness accounts but later fabrications by Jesus' disciples (Google A.I.). These and other views have influenced societal thought and even filtered into the Church of Christ.

Some misconceptions about Jesus Christ and the Christian faith include:

- Jesus' race and appearance: A prevalent misconception, especially portrayed in movies, is that Jesus was a handsome, white European. He was a Jewish man from the Middle East, where the skin tones of the people are diverse.
- His divinity: Some believe Jesus was only a prophet or a powerful human, not fully divine.
- His humanity: While fully divine, Jesus was also fully human and experienced human emotions like anger, sadness, and anxiety. The misconception that He was only a fallible human being is incorrect; He was a human without sin, according to Christian belief.
- Jesus' teachings can be aligned with modern politics; He was a revolutionary on a political mission. The belief that Jesus can be co-opted by any political party is a mischaracterization of His radical, otherworldly message of the Kingdom of God.
- A figure for a single political party. His message of salvation and freedom transcends modern political ideologies, whether liberal or conservative.

- That Jesus' teachings focused on wealth and success through faith is incorrect. The prosperity gospel, which teaches this, is seen as a form of materialism that prioritizes wealth over true spiritual growth, which the Gospel is fundamentally about.
- Individual spirituality can replace the church. The idea that "all we need is Jesus" and that a faith community is unnecessary is a misconception that fuels individualism. The New Testament emphasizes the importance of the church as a body of believers for spiritual growth, accountability, and support.
- A passive, meek figure: While Jesus was gentle and tender, He was also firm in His message of justice and equity, not a passive or easily manipulated figure. (Google A.I.).

My aim through this book was to highlight some of these misconceptions about Jesus Christ and dispel them by making His story clear. I'm defending the faith. Hopefully, those who disbelieve will now believe, and those who have professed faith but have been misled will follow Jesus Christ again without fear. Hopefully, too, the local church will recognize the error of its ways and return to exalting Jesus Christ.

Jesus helped many people and did amazing things because He put God first, trusted the Holy Spirit, prayed often, and remained true to Himself and His teachings, even when facing trouble, betrayal, and enemies. He was consistent. John 21:24-25 tells us, *"... There are many other things that Jesus did. If every one of them were written down, I suppose the whole world would not have room for the books that would be written."* Wow! What more could He have done?

As we have just read about what Jesus did, He never emphasized reason, self-reliance, or independent thinking; He defied science and the natural world, questioned traditional authority, and showed that humanity could be improved through Him alone, changing a person's heart, from where all evil comes. OMG!

He always did/does good and deserves our thanks, as Gospel recording artist Judith McAllister tells us. Listen at https://youtu.be/LDU-H3az1lk?si=aaD5tJ0s0g76Fctn.

Chapter 7 - Jesus' Call: "Follow Me" "I Will Make You…" "Fishers of Men"

Then Jesus said to all of them, If anyone would come after Me, he must deny himself and take up his cross daily and follow Me. For whoever wants to save his life will lose it, but whoever loses his life for My sake will save it. What will it profit a man if he gains the entire world, yet loses or forfeits his very self? (Luke 9:23-25 SB)

If this all resonates with you, you may think, "I'm not yet a follower, but after hearing some of these things about Jesus, I desire to be. What do I need to do? What does being called by Jesus imply? And how will I know it's Him calling me?" Or perhaps you're reflecting, "I once accepted a call to receive Jesus Christ into my life, but nothing more has happened; I'm the same as I was." These questions lead us to consider how people experience Jesus' call.

****

Well, there is no *single, systematic way* Jesus calls someone to salvation—it may differ from the testimonies you've heard from others. While Jesus Christ is the only way to God, how He may bring someone to Him varies. In another chapter, I described how I was called by God as a teenager, during a church sermon, after growing up in a Christian family and regularly reading the Bible. Many established churches invite people to come forward to receive Jesus Christ, which may be how He calls you. Or, like Paul, you might be alone, where no one is around, and the Lord may speak to your heart about your need for Him.

Let's look at how Jesus called His first followers. It's no coincidence that Jesus' interactions with and call to them are in Scripture, although it's the least talked about or followed in Christendom. Jesus strategically selected and approached a team of twelve men to follow Him. They didn't realize it then, but they would play a key role in helping Him achieve His purpose, share His message, and continue His work after He was gone. Jesus was wise enough to know He could not fulfill His life's mission by Himself. He needed witnesses who would spread the word and continue what He started. By imparting His attributes onto them, teaching them, and showing them God's ways, these twelve men would be witnesses to Jesus' life and ministry. They would witness how life was like with Him and later share or record their experience for others to believe. The world would need to hear Jesus' message. Think of them as a pay-it-forward team (you got it, now pass it on). Jesus Christ was only one man and couldn't travel the entire world to spread His message. Those He calls will do that.

To better understand their role, they are known as Jesus Christ's disciples. By divine providence, Jesus chose and established close relationships with these twelve men. Jesus chose these twelve for a specific purpose, even though he had other disciples. I learned years ago at the School of Tyrannus—taught by my brother—that a disciple is "one who goes the same way as another." As disciples of Christ, we follow the way Jesus Christ went and do what He did. We follow His lead. You cannot effectively follow what you do not study with the eyes or hear with the ears. The writings about Jesus' experience with these men should give us some essential principles to employ in our local churches.

The Gospels of Matthew, Mark, Luke, and John record who the disciples were. Matthew 4:18-22 (ESV) describes his initial encounter with some of them. The passage says: *While walking by the Sea of Galilee, he saw two brothers, Simon (who is called Peter) and Andrew, his brother, casting a net into the sea, for they were fishermen. He said to them, "Follow me, and I will make you fishers of men." Immediately, they left their nets and followed him. Continuing on, he saw two other brothers—James, the son of Zebedee, and John, his brother—who were in the boat with Zebedee, their father, mending their nets; he called them as well. Immediately, they left the boat and their father and followed him.*

A similar moment occurred for another disciple, Matthew. In Matthew 9:9 (NIV), it says, *As Jesus went on from there, he saw a man named Matthew sitting at the tax collector's booth. He tells him, "Follow me," and Matthew got up and followed Him.* Also, Mark 2:13-14 mentions Matthew, also known as Levi, son of Alphaeus.

Matthew 10:2-4 lists the names of the other disciples. All of them are: Simon, who is called Peter, and Andrew, his brother; James, the son of Zebedee, and John, his brother; Philip and Bartholomew; Thomas and Matthew (aka Levi), the tax collector; James, the son of Alphaeus, and Thaddaeus; Simon, a Zealot, and Judas Iscariot, who betrayed him. These are the twelve I refer to as Jesus' launch team. He called these guys into a close and personal relationship with Himself by simply saying, *Follow me*. This proves that Jesus' call is for those from different walks of life.

"Follow Me"

We may wonder, "What was it about these guys that Jesus selected them, and what would be required of them?" Are they righteous, morally good guys, law-abiding citizens, well put together, or sinless? Were they handsome, strong, or did they have some type of "swag" about them? Were they wise, intellectual, or well-educated? What was it about them that Jesus picked these men?

It amazes me how the scripture says most of them *instantaneously* left what they were doing to follow Jesus. This leads us to wonder. What was it about Jesus that prompted such a response? According to Isaiah 53:2 in the Bible, Jesus wasn't good-looking: *"He had no beauty or majesty to attract us to Him,"* the scripture says. This differs from what we might expect since physical appearance is so important today. Scripture clarifies that His appearance was ordinary. Media depictions often mislead us, but the reality is different. Jesus wasn't handsome, didn't have impressive stateliness or regal bearing; He was approachable and did not act as if He was above others.

We can imagine that since Jesus wasn't physically attractive, people today might find him too weird to want to approach or get to know, unlike the popular images on social media. His looks wouldn't gain him many followers or popularity. So, Jesus' physical appearance or grandness was not what attracted these men.

In addition, where exactly were they going, or what would they be doing or required of them? Jesus does not say, "Follow me, and here is why." In fact, He gives no details, no travel plans, no blueprints for them. They received no information. Nor does Jesus set requirements or impose demands on them. He does not overwhelm them with a list of rules or things they must first change. There are no how-tos or dos and don'ts. Neither does He say things like, "You're a sinner." "Stop doing that." "Put that down." "Leave that here." "Change your attitude," or "Change your outfit. "Give that up." None of that. In fact, He makes no judgment calls about them at all. He simply says, *Follow me.* Wow! Do you get a sense of ease in those two words? OMG!

Allow me to pause here and apologize (again) to anyone who was scrutinized, rebuffed, judged, or given a list of instructions from me, other Christians, or a local church when you were only just trying to find Jesus Christ. Okay? Let's continue.

So, these twelve guys started following Jesus. They showed some faith in the simple words Jesus spoke. Jesus had not yet mentioned the plan or the reason for calling them. However, they were about to embark on a stupendous journey to witness and experience God the Father in action. They would watch Jesus and see how He used His Father's power, taught, loved, and connected with others through His words and deeds, significantly impacting them. They would hear Jesus' words, learn His ways, and be transformed, and then they would follow His pattern to do similar things.

Considering how Jesus interacted with His disciples showed me He still calls people today in the same way and for the same reasons. He invites us up close to follow Him, and, for many, it's not always immediate what we may become or do. Jesus seems to suggest with these guys the scripture in Psalm 34:8 we discussed earlier, *Taste and see that the Lord is good.* When we taste someone's cooking, we don't gulp it down in large quantities; we only put a spoonful in our mouths to see if it has a tasty flavor. Jesus' call to follow Him is something like that. We start small and consume more day by day.

The Gospel authors all agree about Jesus' words when He first encountered these men. "Follow me" is a simple yet emphatic command. Those who want to follow Christ can infer something. First, obviously, Jesus sees and knows where you are in life, what you are doing, where you are working, and He wants you. His command is for you to watch, pay attention, and study Him. The command was personal to these guys, yet open. He approached them individually, as He does us. Second, Jesus was inviting them to come close into His sphere of being. The door was open for them to get to personally know Jesus, to walk and travel with Him, dine with Him, sleep where He slept, communicate with Him, and observe Him as He ministered to people. He wanted them up close.

These are the only recorded words Jesus spoke to them upon their first encounter. In a nutshell, Jesus' saying "follow me" was an open door for these twelve guys to "Come. Watch. Do what I do." That is precisely what a disciple does. This biblical mandate to "follow me" has remained unchanged. Jesus Christ's call to non-believers, now by the Holy Spirit, is still, *Follow me.* Put your faith in Jesus, watch and learn His ways, and follow Him. Simple. OMG!

Place Yourself in this Story

Imagine Jesus being present in this century. It's your most ordinary day. You are working at your desk, typing a memorandum for the boss, and you need to distribute it to the Public Relations Department staff by 5:00 pm. The phones are ringing unusually high today, and customers are steadily flowing in and out of the office. As the front desk receptionist, you're the initial contact. You must always remain cordial, composed, and professional when customers arrive or call. You should be polite and helpful.

It's 3 pm, and you still haven't begun typing the memo. You're getting stressed a bit and lament with a deep sigh, grumbling under your breath, "Where are all these people coming from today?" By 3:30 pm, things subside enough so that you can begin typing the memo. Although the memo is short, you must type, proofread, send it for review and approval, print, get it signed, run copies, and distribute it to the staff. "No emails," the boss emphasizes. "Only hard copies should go out." "Ugh!" You're steadily striking the computer keys while intermittently watching the front door.

It's now 3:55 pm, and in walks another customer. He's approaching your desk. You mutter another disgruntled complaint, "Oh boy! What does he want at 4 pm? We're about to close." You look up, muster a fake smile, and try to act interested. "Hello, sir. Welcome to the Doe & Doe Company. How may I help you?" The gentleman returns the smile, gestures with his hand, and replies. "Hello, Ms. Parks, right? I am Jesus Christ of Nazareth. Please, follow me."

We may laugh at this scenario in our times, which are so different from those of the Bible, but consider it. Placing ourselves in the text helps us gain a better appreciation for the story and understand the characters' feelings. We rarely imagine Jesus' presence in such modern times, but suppose Jesus were on earth now? It's good to think about sometimes. For each of the twelve disciples, Jesus approached them in this way. They were in the heart of their ordinary day, fishing or working at their jobs. They were engaged in their craft or livelihood, or spending time with their family. We know they were fishermen because it says, "They immediately left their nets." (See Matthew 4:18-22; 8:18-22; 9:9; Mark 1:16-17, 19-20, 2:14.) So, understand, then, that a call to journey with Jesus is *personal* to you and can happen any time, regardless of what you may be doing.

Honestly, considering the times in which we now live, if a human were to walk up and approach me today and say, "Follow me," it would be quite unsettling. I'd think the person was weird, or I would feel under attack and call security. To immediately stop typing the memo, shut down my computer, pack up my desk, and grab my purse to follow Him, I don't know that I would. "What? Who are you?" I'd argue. But this is what the record says these men did upon Jesus' greeting.

Remember, these men were living in troublesome times and belonged to a minority race. They were already facing unfair treatment and living under domination and control. We can be sure they may have had some trust issues and apprehension when Jesus first approached them;

it's human nature.

But *immediately,* the Bible states, they followed Jesus. This causes us to ask, "Why?" I thought about this as I studied the story. What was it about Jesus that made these men drop everything and follow Him? We already established that it wasn't His physical appeal or any societal status he held. Yes, Jesus was of the same race as they, and perhaps this gave them some comfort, but that's not enough to go by. "They left everything," it says; some, even their parents. They may have recognized Jesus from seeing Him at the open market or walking the streets. Perhaps they were familiar with Joseph's carpentry or stone building work, as he did business with them and Jesus. Perhaps their knowledge of the Torah and the prophecies of a Messiah came to mind. Did they recognize Jesus as the Messiah? The record shows one did. In John 1:40-42, Andrew found his brother Simon and said, *We have found the Messiah.* With the others, however, was there a discerning factor at play here? Possibly. Did they immediately believe Him?

Personally, I think something was compelling in Jesus' voice. It was kind, confident, clear, yet authoritative like a leader. It made them feel as if they could trust Him. Jesus' gentle yet authoritative voice caused a reaction in their hearts. They recognized there was something real, different about Him. His words penetrated and touched their entire being. It's like the time I told you about when I heard the Holy Spirit's voice in church; I knew it was real. I knew it was the voice of Jesus.

This may be the way Jesus introduced Himself. Right then, these men knew nothing about Jesus. The scripture does not say Jesus immediately revealed his Messiahship to them. Furthermore, people had not widely known about Jesus yet. He had not started His public ministry. He was not the popular guy everyone wanted to hang out with or hear speak. Stories were not circulating throughout the community about "the new guy on the block performing miracles." So, His saying, *follow me,* and their immediate reaction to do so is *not* because of popularity, charisma, money, or gifts exchanged, healings performed, promises made, or any evidence He showed.

Jesus' command to "follow me" was the *first* and only mandate Jesus gave these twelve guys. It's "an invitational command." It's authoritative, emphatic, compelling, and above you; it's genuine. You recognize it's Jesus calling because your heart will move. You will know! When you say "Yes" and start following, the journey begins!

"I Will Make You …"

Next, we find Jesus explaining to the disciples why He asked them to follow Him. He reveals the reason to these guys at some point. I say it's more of a revelation rather than a command here because Jesus tells them what He's going to do. He says to them, *"I will make you…"* Again, Jesus' words are clear, direct, and authoritative. He does not mince words or put any fluff in them. Jesus lets them know in so many words, "Here's the deal; here's what's going to take place when you follow me." This serves to inform and provide assurance to these men.

Jesus' statement of "I will make you…," is interesting! In saying it, He's putting the full onus of this call on Himself. This is astounding and caused an OMG moment in me when I studied it. Jesus does not say to them here, "Look, I need you to sit at my feet every day for 2-3 hours. I want you to go into the temple and listen to the reading of the scroll every day." Or "I need you to act properly in public with me and stop that behavior because I am Jesus Christ, the Messiah, and I don't want you embarrassing me." None of that. In fact, Jesus doesn't tell them to rid themselves of anything sinful, evil, give up bad habits, or change their personality. In addition, He does not ask them to take part in or practice anything religious or ritualistic. He simply alludes to a change in them that will occur, and He will bring it about. He takes full responsibility for making this change happen. At this juncture, all they had to do was trust this.

What is Jesus going to make of them? And why do they even need to be made over? They're grown men. I'm sure the disciples' eyebrows raised at Jesus' words here, and they had questions. We are funny sometimes when others suggest we need to change something. We're prideful. The disciples may have thought, "Who the heck does He think He is? I'm a fisherman. What is He talking about?" Matthew, the tax collector, may have thought. "I'm fully established, making plenty of money, and living large. Please give me a break! What is he going to make of me? I'm doing fine; I'm cool."

In contrast, Jesus' words here may have frightened some of them. They weren't as self-assured or confident. They may have been introverted. Others may have noticed something good, pure, and genuine about Jesus that wasn't in them. "He's too good to hang out with," they surmise. In another scenario that could have crossed the disciples' minds upon Jesus' saying, "I will make you…" may have been, "Good. Finally! I need a change in my life. He's going to make all my dreams come true." Has anyone ever told you that if you accept Jesus Christ's call, He will give you everything you ever wanted? You won't sin anymore, ever be sick, and He will fill you with total happiness and take away all your problems, pain, and sadness. Jesus never completed His statement with any of these misdirected promises because they are not true when you decide to follow Jesus. Any person, minister, or church proclaiming this as a prophetic word coming from God is lying to you. Continue reading; you'll see why.

Here, we discover the authority the Lord Jesus Christ has in the Christian faith by placing the making of His followers totally in His hands. A scripture in 1 Thessalonians 5:24 (KJV) confirms this. It says, *Faithful is He that calleth you, who also will do it.*

Yes, there is a change that is required when one follows Christ. It begins in your heart and then works itself outward. Jesus Christ will change your heart to think like Himself, to be more like Him, and to act like a Christian. He is going to do this through you. He is going to make this happen as you learn more of Him, get to know Him better, and follow Him.

You allow Him to take control of your life and guide the ship, and He will transform you. There is no need to worry or fret about what's presently wrong or how long it has not been good in your life. Jesus invites His followers not to be weary or fret. You can rest and relax. He's got this. *He is going to change you.*

Exhale!!!

"Fishers of Men"

Remarkably, Jesus' discourse continues; Hreveals *what* He will make of these men. There's a specific purpose in Jesus' call to us. Jesus tells these guys He's going to transform them or make them "fishers of men." This involves what they will become and what they will do. The Lord has something in mind when He calls you.

I'm sure the disciples squinted again at this statement. "What is a fisher of men? I don't know what He means by this. What is He talking about? We catch fish."

This part of Jesus' words is also interesting. He reveals His purpose. He will transform them into something different from their present state, or what they were used to. Followers of Jesus Christ do not live life haphazardly with no purpose. They also do not set their own agendas for their lives. It's what the verse in Luke 9:23 alludes to, where it says, *If anyone would come after me, he must deny himself and take up his cross daily and follow Me.* In our journey with Jesus, the Holy Spirit may challenge us at different seasons to deny ourselves for Him—maybe something, our responses to current affairs or people's predicaments, our wishes, plans, agendas, careers, livelihoods, etc.—whatever it may be. This is different for each of us.

Jesus intends to transform our hearts and minds toward/for people. He is relational and concerned about people. Journeying with Jesus is *not about* changing us to amass wealth, gain material possessions, such as fancy cars, lavish homes, loyal spouses, high-paying jobs, perfect children, or other material things; these are only byproducts of God's blessings that some of you may achieve and some not. They're not Jesus Christ's goal for saving us. We need to stop promoting this; it's not true. OMG!

We noted how Jesus called these individuals to follow Him while they were engaged in their daily work. Most of the disciples were skilled fishermen, expeditious in their trade. Every day, they caught fish and may have sold them at the marketplace or eaten them at home for dinner. The other, Matthew, a tax collector, surely understood the fishing business because he collected taxes on it. Simon, a Zealot, was involved in politics (Matthew 9:9).

The point is that Jesus met and welcomed these men to follow Him, accepting them as they were, in their occupations, careers, or life pursuits. His statement, "... make you fishers of men," proves that there is a purpose when one is chosen to follow Christ. It involves developing a heart for people. Jesus would transform their zeal for natural things into spiritual matters.

Jesus would expand their understanding from catching fish to catching people. As fishermen, they knew how to bait the hook, chum the waters, jig the line, prepare the nets, or steer the boat to locations where the fish were; they knew the best times to fish. They knew how to operate their business for profit.

The keyword here is *transformation.* Jesus' call involves a change. He changes us, transforms us into the person to be used in God's eternal kingdom. This is what Jesus was saying to the disciples here, employing the very craft that they loved. He used what they knew and loved to drive home the idea of catching people now. Jesus would transform these men's zeal for catching fish for profit into a zeal for catching people for God's kingdom. Did they immediately understand? Probably not. Did they immediately know who, what, where, and how? Probably not. Did they immediately have the heart for people? Probably not. However, as they continued to pay attention to Jesus—listening to and watching His interactions with people and how He cared for them—in time, their hearts would become filled with the same enthusiasm. As they continued traveling with Jesus, people would become their priority, too. They witnessed how much Jesus cared for, loved, and invested in people. People would take precedence over all they had known and been their whole lives.

I think that in this statement, Jesus describes His mission to His twelve disciples and all followers after them. He transforms our hearts from a self-focused, self-directed, and self-centered focus to a God-centered heart, which is focused on people.

Here, Jesus is acting just like the Father, God in the OT, who often interrupted the lives of the prophets or leaders He called. He told them to do perplexing things they didn't always immediately understand, such as when He told Abraham to take his only son and sacrifice him on the altar. Or when He told Moses to stand at the Red Sea and put out his rod over the waters so the sea could part and the Israelites could cross. How have we come today to make God so predictable? OMG!

The men may have initially debunked Jesus' words. They may have had a twinge of fear. I recall reading certain words in scripture that caused me to fear. "I hope He doesn't ask that of me," I'd think. It's human nature to be skeptical of those we first meet. Regardless of how many others may have told us about someone's niceness, we still want to discover it for ourselves. We are unlikely to trust someone right away. Also remember, these are just men. Were they offended at His suggestion of minimizing their love for fish? Did egos flare about being transformed into something other than what they were? We take pride in our skill. "Catch men? I don't even like or get along with people, especially certain types," we may think.

Jesus telling these men He was going to make them "fishers of men" is significant for understanding how God has a will for us when Jesus saves us. I call this *the invitational change*. Jesus Christ's call to deny ourselves means He wants to take first place in our lives after receiving Him. Jesus is direct here and again uses no tricky words, gimmicks, ploys, or sales pitches. He does not tell them their fishing business will prosper more if they include people in the paradigm. He doesn't even ask them to leave their fishing business altogether. Nope.

Jesus captures their attention by employing language that was of interest or unique to them. He used what they knew, understood, and loved so they could grasp is point of view (or vision). We can be sure that after making this statement, the entire process that goes into catching fish caused these men to think about people.

Most of us like to think of ourselves as good people who care. Maybe on a natural level, we are and do our best. Jesus' call for change is spiritual, not only about helping people. He wants us to love them the way He does, and bring them into a relationship with God, the Father, like He did or will do for you. Paying it forward.

This is the reason Jesus Christ came into the world, as stated in John 3:16. Catching people and reeling them in for Christ. This is the sole mission for which we are called and saved by Jesus Christ, and it requires a change from what's on our heart to what's on God's heart—which is people. He's not willing that any should perish; He chose us as His representatives so they wouldn't, and

Jesus has taken full responsibility for making this happen through us.

The Takeaway

Interestingly, it didn't happen this way for me. Up to a certain point in my life, I, too, had only just received Christ into my life, and that was it. My "fishers of men" call or a call to surrender my life to Christ happened much later. (I'll tell you how; continue reading.)

One's journey with Christ begins by first believing His message and receiving Him into one's heart. We pay attention to Jesus and follow Him as our leader, the teacher, the preeminent One. We attend church, read about Him in Scripture, learn His ways, and begin taking our cues from Him (or should, anyway). Second, following Jesus will cause a life change—some immediate, some later. We trust Jesus for this change and try not to exert our strength or effort trying to do it ourselves.

Our opening verse clarifies what following Jesus means. The word "would" is the past future tense of "will," signifying if a person "will come" after Jesus, they must deny themselves, which is what the disciples were being asked to do, and all Christ followers after them. To transform your priorities/passions into God's passion. To exchange what you love or are enthusiastic about for what God loves. That's an example of denying oneself or losing one's life. For some, this may alter your entire personality, way of thinking, approach to life, career pursuits, social circle, living arrangements, travel habits, or worldview—not your gender. Jesus approached and chose the twelve, no matter their careers, livelihoods, or earthly pursuits. It was not immediately known all this would mean. But they trusted that the whole onus of their transformation and sanctification was on Christ, not them. He would do it, He said. They simply had to follow. As a result, their yes to Jesus transformed them into the greatest, most loyal, and boldest evangelists the world has ever known. (See the book of Acts.)

Today, as a follower of Christ, expect that at some point, the Lord will challenge your heart for people. So, expect this. The Lord will change your stony heart, shifting your focus from yourself to others. Don't think about the hundreds or thousands like Jesus affected; start with the one He'll lead you to. You'll want them to find what you found when you met Jesus. Some things you have been through, struggles or failures you've had, or a hurt you experienced is for you to tell (or testify) to one person. Why? They are experiencing the same thing—without Jesus.

Karl Barth on Election

Theologian Karl Barth, in Christian Dogmatics, Volume II, discusses the doctrine of God's election. He terms the doctrine of election as the "election of grace," noting that it is God's gracious nature of love and through freedom that He has elected humankind for salvation. Barth states, "It is certain that this election is a work in which God meets the world neither in indifference nor in enmity, but in which at the very highest and lowest levels (in the giving of His only begotten Son) He is for this man Jesus, and in Him for the whole race, and therefore for the world. That God wills neither to be without the world nor against it can never be stated more clearly or forcibly than when we speak of His election," (Barth).

John 3:17 (NIV) supports Barth's thinking on this point. It says, *For God did not send his Son into the world to condemn the world, but to save the world through Him.*

Barth continues, "The election of grace is the sum of the Gospel—we must put it as pointedly as that. But more, the election of grace is the whole of the Gospel, the Gospel in nuce. It is the very essence of all good news. It must be understood and evaluated in the Christian Church. God is God in His being as One who loves in freedom... It is itself evangel: glad tidings; good news; news which uplifts, comforts, and sustains" (Barth).

God elected us to be called through Jesus Christ, just as Jesus selected His twelve disciples. You do not get elected by winning a majority vote. Strategically and intentionally, God selects us to contribute to His plan of salvation for the world—to pay it forward.

For by grace you have been saved through faith. And this is not your own doing; it is the gift of God, not a result of works, so that no one may boast (Ephesians 2:8-9 ESV).

Isn't this outstanding? It's incredibly simple. Why are we stressed so much?

Wow!

Chapter 8 - Forbidden Fruit, Demon Spirits, Panic Attacks - Oh My!

Life kept moving on for me, and I enjoyed Christ's presence—until those feelings faded. My joy vanished, and temptations I'd never faced before surfaced. I found an appeal in them. Others indulging in these activities seemed to be okay; they weren't facing any negative consequences. So, I was curious, followed the crowd, and gave in to sin. Even bolder temptations emerged, and I fell for the allure and reluctantly ate from the forbidden tree. Aww, man!

I say reluctantly because you know that what you're doing is incorrect. This proves Jesus Christ saved you; His Holy Spirit within alerts you. (More about the Holy Spirit soon. Continue reading.) After you sin, conviction follows. But if you persist, it feels good and exciting. You develop a liking and keep going. Don't expect either your non-Christian friends to stop you; they won't. They'll continue saying, "Come on," and pass you the joint, or pour you a drink, or say, "Just lie down and relax."

Yes, those proclivities that all humans have and that appeal to our natural appetites surfaced inside of me—the appetites for fortune (get rich), fame (become known), power (gain control), and pleasure (be satisfied). It's true; these appetites are inside us. I learned the hard way to never say, "I'll never..."

I was just having fun and finding glee in negative activities. As I grew bolder, sin became routine. Earthly fun replaced my joy. There's a difference between joy from Jesus and worldly happiness.

There was a neighborhood group I spent time with (about ten of us). We were young and curious, trying different activities. Neighborhood kids were more social then, and we would often visit each other's homes. Our parents knew each other and communicated, and there was more trust in the neighborhood than there is now. We didn't feel the need to scrutinize people and situations as much. These friends were peers from school or my community. Most often, I visited their homes because nothing sinful would happen in mine. They knew it, and so did I. I had to keep things hidden, and I did.

Because of the lifestyle I chose, I graduated from high school a year late. I wanted to attend Howard University for journalism, but no one encouraged me to pursue it, and the desire eventually waned. I attempted courses at the local community college but never finished. I was smart but misdirected and, yes, also stupid at times. My father liked that I was smart and often reminded me of it. He liked my initiative and business acumen. He was a loyal, hard worker for a chemical plant. He did shift work and rarely missed a day. But again, I don't recall any family members or teachers encouraging me to develop myself or my talents and gifts. Getting a college degree was my desire and stayed in my heart, but I had issues—low self-esteem, body image issues, personality quirks, trying to be cool and fit in somewhere, and searching for acceptance. This went on for a while, shaping much of what was to come next.

Acceptance is a natural human need we all have. In his WordPress blog "We're Glad You're Here," Pastor Virgil Stokes, Founding Pastor of Goodness Family Church in Tucson, Arizona, discussed this issue. (You can read his blog at https://pastorvirgil.com/2025/08/02/were-glad-youre-here/). I loved the blog because it included the theme song from the Cheers television sitcom. I watched that show and liked the song. I actually enjoyed and watched several television shows where friendship was highlighted. Pastor Virgil also remembered the Cheers theme song. The lyrics say, "*Sometimes you wanna go where everybody knows your name, and they're always glad you came. You want to be where you can see; our troubles are all the same. You want to be where everybody knows your name*." It's true, isn't it? We want to be liked, accepted, and to have nice friends who accept us. Pastor Virgil writes on his blog, "When I was a kid, one of my favorite places in the world was my grandmother's bar and truck stop. I liked having an endless supply of soda, peanuts, and candy bars. I also liked to shoot pool and play the jukebox for free. But the big attraction for a really shy kid like me was the feeling of being completely accepted. I even had a nickname: Shorty" (Stokes). Although the show focused on people who were close friends in a bar, the idea of being known, accepted, and liked is the key here. I felt this way with the group of people I hung out with; most of them seemed to enjoy having me around. (Only one seemed not to.) Everybody called me "Ellie." Pastor Virgil concludes, however, "For all my Christian life, I have asked the question, 'Wouldn't it be wonderful if I felt as accepted in church as I did in Grandma's tavern?' (Stokes). Good point he makes, huh? I started this book by saying, "No one noticed." Why aren't people feeling accepted in Jesus Christ's Church? What's happening? OMG!

In addition, overwhelming trials and sadness ensued in my family. Life took another turn: there was indescribable family separation and pain—mental breakdowns, sickness, financial hardships, parents' separation, and Mom struggling to keep us afloat.

My heart shattered when things began to change. This depressed me, heightened my anxiety, and made me sad, along with the lifestyle I got caught up in. I confessed, prayed, and kept moving. But my attitude became negative, my mouth disrespectful, and fear and anxiety plagued me. I was confused, angry, and cussing and fussing inside. "Oh, no!" I thought. "My wonderful Christian experience with Jesus is shattered, has disappeared, and is ended." This is how I felt. Disappointed. Bewildered. Confused. I look up, and in much perplexity, lament, "But I thought...?"

Jesus Christ is Still There

I used to wish my experience was like that of other Christians I talked to, who told me everything changed the moment they received Christ. They immediately gave up their old attitudes, stopped unpleasant habits, began serving in the church, or recognized a specific ministry Christ was calling them to. Things didn't go this way for me.

I recall a time when my mother asked me, "What is it?" She asked because of my mouth. I frequently backtalked and disrespected her with loud, unpleasant outbursts. As I later reflected on these outbursts, they were words that did not reflect what was in my heart for my mother; I loved her and held her in high esteem. I don't know what was wrong with me then that made me say such things to her. I responded to my mother. "It's a spirit." I knew nothing about spirits, nor had I studied them in the Scriptures. But this came out of my mouth to tell my mom what was happening to me. As I think about my life foibles, there *was* some type of oppressive spirit constantly plaguing me to keep me bound, anxious, fearful, and with low self-esteem. I saw this spirit once, for real, in my bedroom.

Demonic/Oppressive Spirits

This encounter with a demonic spirit was brief but memorable and scared the daylights out of me. I was lying in bed, under the blankets, positioned to fall asleep. As I turned my body to lie on my back, I looked up, and suddenly there it was—an evil, strong-looking figure in all black hovering over me. I gasped in shock and fear and quickly pulled up the blanket to cover my eyes. After a few moments, I lowered the blanket to look again, and the figure was gone. I don't recall praying this time or calling out, "Jesus!" Whenever I was afraid or having one of my panic attacks, I usually did. I just deeply breathed in and exhaled, thinking, "What the heck was that?" I finally drifted off to sleep.

Another oppressive event in my life occurred on Thanksgiving Day. I was in the same room, but this time lying on the bed, paralyzed in fear. I felt as if I were sick and about to die any minute. (This is something the enemy constantly bothered me about—sickness and dying.) I was a hypochondriac who feared sickness so much that I feared going to the doctor. Crazy thoughts were racing through my mind, and my heart was pounding so much that my entire body went limp; I could not move. I felt crazy and was acting as if I were feeble because it felt so real. My sister, Carol, peered in the doorway. Compassionately, she looked at me and said, "Aww, are you okay?" She noticed something awry in me. I must have looked like I was in some kind of trouble to her because she stepped into my room. I don't recall exactly how I explained to Carol how I was feeling, but I talked to her. I don't remember either the exact words she said to me or the prayers she prayed, if any. (I'm sure she did.) We just chatted. What I do remember is how I felt after talking with her. Such a surge of energy and vigor went through my body that I could stand on my feet. I walked out of that room with my sister, recovered and ready to eat a wonderful Thanksgiving dinner with my family. I'll never forget that day; it was strange, but proof to me that oppressive spirits are real.

Lastly, anxiety, negative self-talk, depression, and body image issues were other problems I had in my life. Anxiety is something I've always had. Even today, it still surfaces, although not as intensely. I cannot count the times when a panic attack struck me out of nowhere. Panic attacks can be very severe. You want to take off running, just pass out, or die because the negative thoughts are racing in your head; they seem so real. Nonstop, one negative thought after another, plagues your mind. You feel as if you have no control and are about to lose your mind. Your heart races, too. You're sweating and pacing the floor. You have a sense of impending danger that is about to overtake you. I would entertain these attacks with my negative self-talk. Most of the time, the words I said or the names I called myself had to do with a previous sin I had committed. I thought God was mad and coming after me to punish me. I also used to think God was angry with me whenever there was a thunderstorm with lightning. LOL.

Few would recognize the anxiety and fear that plagued me because of the way I carried myself. I exude such confidence, energy, and positivity. Those closest to me would notice it. But for much of my life, I've had to ward off anxious thoughts or feelings and negative self-talk. Although others made me aware that I was talking negatively and putting myself down, I didn't hear it. It was years before I learned to fight those thoughts by praying and using God's Word. Even now, I must check my thoughts and monitor my self-talk.

I cannot tell you how many days and hours I lay awake having a panic attack, being afraid, thinking negative thoughts, or talking negatively to myself. I would find Scriptures to read, usually a Psalm, and read them aloud to myself or pray them. I also found videos with worship songs or prayers to rout these demonic and oppressive spirits. Many nights, I finally drifted off to sleep in the wee hours of the morning because the oppressive experience lasted long. It's a horrible malady to have.

Depression, too, is another spirit that would engulf me at times. I recall a time when I was living in a friend's home and was very depressed. I did not know anyone in this neighborhood. Again, I was not sick, but the loneliness and sadness I felt were real, so much so that I felt intense pain in my stomach. Oh, it was bad! I would run to the door, hoping someone would visit to talk to me. No one ever came. But the Lord spoke to me one day to get up out of bed and begin walking outside. Little by little, the depression lifted.

Body Image Issues

My body image issues primarily concerned my feet, height, and body shape. I have noticeably big, long feet, long arms, and legs. (Message me and I'll tell you my shoe size. LOL.) I always thought my figure was more masculine than feminine. I don't have one of those hourglass figures. As I matured and accepted what I have, I realized this came from my tall Dad, who was over 6 feet; my mother was only about 5'3'. I'm about 5'9" now. Before my acceptance, I cannot tell you the countless days I spent comparing myself to other women. At the pool, gym, the park, or wherever, I sat comparing my feet and body to theirs. I'd think, "There is no other woman who has feet or a body like this." I spent days berating my feet and body until Mom, I guess, became tired of hearing me do so. She yelled, "Ellie, those are your feet, and you're going to have to accept them." One notable thing about my body image issues is that although I thought I had more male features than a woman's, I never thought I was a man or desired to be one. Thank the Lord for showing me Psalm 139! Woohoo! 😊 Check it out.

Most of the spirits I've dealt with, hang-ups I've had, or ways I've reacted, had a root in how I felt about myself: my looks, personality, bad decisions, or always feeling God felt bad about me too and was only out to whack me. The Lord proved to me that this was not true; that's why I love Him today. Through every sin, attack, oppressive experience, depression, or the negative way I thought about myself, He always gently lifted me out of it. Where we read that prophecy in Isaiah about Jesus that says, "*The Spirit of the Lord is on me, because he has anointed me ... to set the oppressed free...*" It's really true. He did it for me. I'm a witness!

Despite all my challenges: the misdirection, striving, struggle, trial and error, and peaks and valleys, I do not know how, but I knew Christ was still inside me. I knew neither that all of this was leading to my transformation into a fisher of men.

A Single Mom

I was never a "girlie" type girl. I was never heavily focused on marriage or having children, possibly because I thought no one would want to marry me or because I was not too in touch with my feminine side. The bows, flowers, ribbons, makeup, or fashion women love were never heavily a part of me. Don't get me wrong, I think these things are beautiful, and I like them. I just invest a little time or money in them. I'm a head kind of girl. Now, if you put me in front of a computer or give me a desktop publishing job, a proposal to write, a business plan to think about or prepare, or a tech problem to solve, I'm over the top.

So, I dated several nice guys and fell in love often (so I thought). However, I had an uncanny ability to know when I was dating someone who wasn't that into me. They didn't genuinely care about or love me. I know now, but not always back then, how guys all along are showing you their true feelings for you—whether we girls want to admit it. This was the hardest lesson Mom had to drill into me about chasing a man — "Don't do it." I was a chaser and thought if I caught them, I could make a guy love me. In fact, it was the Lord who showed me later in life how my giving in sexually to a man was based on a need in me for acceptance. It wasn't because I was so hot for sex. I was pleading with them to stay with me. I finally put things together and learned that you do not have to give in or defy your morals when a guy loves you. When they are into you, they are enthusiastic, on time, move, hunt, or prowl—usually quick and with intensity. They wait for you. I think women need to stop spending so much time discussing breakups or what happened with the men in their lives. "He didn't love me" is my only story now. That's it.

I went through this pleading cycle for acceptance with a few guys in my life and became pregnant at age 24. By this time, I was a member of a Baptist church, with a loving pastor and his wife; they did not judge me but offered invaluable advice and supported me. The pastor encouraged me to go on with my life and concentrate on my child. (Yes, I followed my brother here also. LOL).

I gave birth to a wonderful son, Bryant Michael. He's my only child. I did not marry this guy, so I was a single parent and responsible for Bryant's care. I never saw myself as mother material. This stemmed from being out of touch with my female side, or how my view of femininity differed from the stereotypes. I was the type of woman who liked to go, be busy, and keep moving. Because I wasn't "girly," being a mother was something I didn't think I would excel at. Although I disappointed my Christian self to get pregnant without a husband, I'm happy I did not choose to have an abortion. Talk about God causing all things to work out for good. The changes, growth, and maturity that occurred in my life after I became a mom were phenomenal. I'm still amazed at how the Lord stayed with me during this time and taught me how to be a mom. I knew nothing about it. I was somewhat of a tomboy and spent more time around men than women. I was self-centered and consumed with being successful in life, too. Surely these were not good motherly virtues. The Lord surprised me, however.

I still ask my son from time to time today, "Did I ever appear out of touch or as if I wasn't listening to you or was brushing you off or rejecting you?" I ask because that's how self-absorbed I was when I gave birth to him. However, the Lord did not abandon me in the task but proved Himself faithful and taught me how to be a mom. He showed me what to do and how to do it. He provided me with good jobs. He taught me how to instill the Scriptures in Bryant's life through practical, everyday lessons on his level, in our home, or wherever we went. Listening to and watching myself instruct my son amazed me. I knew it was only coming from the Lord's help.

I wasn't a perfect single mom, nor was the task easy, but I recognized the seriousness of the role and the sacrifices it would entail. I think that when becoming a mother, one must take a back seat to oneself. You must mature and realize that another human now depends on you. You must let go of some “bad” things you may do or negative attitudes you hold. A child doesn’t need to be exposed to certain things, so you shouldn’t be involved in them. Also, you can’t suddenly decide to aggressively pursue your goals, like going to college to get a degree that you should have gotten before a kid got here. This is my opinion. I think working *and* trying to earn a degree while raising a new child is selfish. You will neglect the child because you will be away from him/her a lot.

I waited to get my long-desired bachelor’s degree. I could have completed college after high school, but I didn’t take advantage of the freedom I had. When it came to my mind to pursue college when Bryant was little, I told myself, “You had all the time in the world before Bryant was born to do whatever you wanted. Why pursue that now? Concentrate on him.” So, I didn’t go to school until later, but I continued working. My advice is to work to maintain a pleasant home for your child and pay the bills so that you can spend quality time with them. Working, schoolwork, and household management take up much of parents’ time, leaving little for kids. I am aware this isn’t always possible for every single mom, so ask the Lord to show you what He wants you to do. That’s just a tip from me.

These are the mature, unselfish decisions you must make as a parent. You realize that this little person in your life now knows nothing. You must nurture them and help them grow in every way: physically, emotionally, mentally, and spiritually. The prenatal classes educate mothers about the physical aspects of pregnancy and childbirth. We need this. However, women could benefit from classes on best practices to prepare themselves emotionally and mentally, so they’re ready when the child arrives. We want to nurture and develop whole human beings, so we should strive to be whole ourselves, to the best of our ability, to begin and continue this lifelong task, not perfectly, but effectively.

Ironically, I discovered, as many mothers told me, that those motherly instincts do kick in after you have a child. I awoke on time, became gentler and more aware, and had Bryant’s bottles and food ready on time. As he grew up, I also noticed that my personality was not so bad for raising a son. With the high energy I had, I’d play sports with him. If he were skateboarding, I would try it too. If he played softball, I would be up to bat next. We took long country drives, walked around the park, and swam, a lot. Turns out, my personality worked out well for a boy.

The best I could do was pass on to him the same spiritual awareness I gained as a kid. I did so to ensure he would become a respectful, productive, industrious, godly citizen in society. Thank the Lord he is. In fact, I noticed Bryant was godlier than I at an early age. He said or did things that made me do a double take at him. Or I remember the times he would give me a specific look when he saw me doing something inconsistent with being a Christian. He looked at me as if to say, "You're not supposed to be doing that, Mom." He was young, and I'd think, "How do you know about this?" If we're not too prideful, we should give our kids their props when they're right about our flaws and biases.

Conclusion

Through all my negative experiences and personality flaws, I later discovered how the Bible is true when it says in John 10:10 (ESV), *The thief comes only to steal and kill and destroy; I have come that they may have life and have it to the full.* Feeling needy, wanting to fit in, hating yourself, being depressed, worrying excessively about anything, giving in to others, disrespecting your parents, having panic attacks, and fear don't lead to a full and meaningful life. God's beloved children might experience these things, but they are not supposed to stay and defeat us.

There is also a counterattack Scripture verse we can use against the devil, who has stolen some time or goodness from us. If, like me, you've made some blunders, have personality disorders or issues, deal with oppressive spirits that want you down and out, or you lost some time doing foolish things, read Romans 8:28 (NIV) that says, *And we know that in all things God works for the good of those who love him, who have been called according to his purpose.*

You're saying, "But you don't know how bad life was/is for me?" Well, **all things mean *all* things**. OMG!

God, who is always good, will make something good out of your bad.

Chapter 9 - My "Fishers of Men" Story

I share some of my personal testimony with you to show that salvation in Christ does not guarantee a life free from problems, even a struggle against sin. As long as we are in this life, we still wrestle with our sinful nature, face spiritual battles, have personality struggles, and fall short. The crucial point I've discovered is that after you accept the Lord Jesus Christ, He's not like humankind and stays with you, continuously pursuing you. He does not abandon us, put up His nose at us, or "kick us to the curb." Like He didn't His twelve disciples.

In the global church today, I notice that discipleship—the call from Jesus Christ to become transformed followers—is fading from focus. They seldom highlight the importance of being a disciple, judging by what I hear from believers in Christ and what I see in churches. It's almost as if Jesus didn't want this to be an important aspect of God's plan. This is crucial because missing this point leads us away from Christ's intent. God, including in the Biblical accounts the disciples' experience with Jesus, is not just a great story; there are important principles we should follow. OMG!

Not all churches are at fault, but many are operating as independent entities or as a business rather than as one unified body focused on Christ. This results in teaching that prioritizes church programs or self-help over Jesus' methods and message. For some, following tradition is more important than following Jesus, which can make activities feel less genuine. The core problem is that churches often focus on themselves rather than on Jesus Christ.

No one fully understands the kingdom of light God brings us into when Jesus saves us. We start the journey and bit by bit, as the Lord uncovers it in our daily life circumstances, we learn. Several may not even be aware that God is transitioning (or making) us. Churches are not teaching this but rather are promoting a self-reliance or do-it-yourself type of gospel. We moved from darkness into a kingdom of light and think and live now the way God views us. Instead, new believers are being oriented to think and act like the church and its members, rather than Jesus Christ.

It happened to me at the church where Jesus Christ saved me. There was no follow-up about what had just taken place. I received no invitation to join a class about *salvation in Jesus Christ* or to learn more about who He is. I have joined churches where I was required to attend a new member's class, but these primarily orient new members to that church's philosophy, protocols, ministry, and activities. A questionnaire might ask if someone is a Christian or if they accepted Jesus Christ, and that's it; they don't even confirm this. It's a very brief acknowledgment.

While some churches teach discipleship and transformation, it's not a priority in others. Early Christians, despite their flaws, always focused their faith on Jesus Christ, including their worship, sharing, and mutual support. This strong focus sets them apart from us, and a comparison with them and today's church raises a question: Have we lost sight of what they understood?

Given these concerns, local churches should provide foundational classes for new Christians. This would help people of faith by leading them to think like Christ, make godly choices, and find their purpose. Churches can play a key role in fostering discipleship from the beginning.

I do not blame the church where I received salvation. Based on all I've shared, you shouldn't blame the people or place that led you to the Lord. Most likely, they didn't know either.

It helped that my parents and siblings were Christian preachers, teachers, or educators. I could ask questions. I followed each one of them, and at different periods was especially close to each of them. They always hosted Christian events—gatherings, retreats, musical programs, preaching engagements, or fun outings. My siblings had a singing group too, and we often performed at church functions. This kept me connected to the church and God. It was a blessing, although I didn't always see it that way when I was trying to fit in. Such a family led to my transformation, which wasn't immediate or as I expected.

Keep Going, Regardless

Despite your struggles, stay involved in church. Remember that Christ is within you—always. I prayed a lot during my struggles. I remember the days, weeks, and months that I cried out to God about the evil in my life or my personality struggles. I'd confess my wrongs and ask Him to take them away often. I'd lie prostrate on the floor, weeping about my negative ways, thoughts, and feelings that I knew didn't line up with His. I prayed earnestly, fasted, and wept over what wasn't Christlike in me. Most times, the Lord's answer was just silence; He said nothing. I didn't get any guidance, criticism, or confirmation that I was mistaken, only silence. Later, God would speak to me about a particular sin in my life. I learned from this how to be quiet sometimes with others who may struggle with a particular sin. (It is not always necessary to offer a comment, a reprimand, or suggestions.) I learned I can go to prayer for them to God, the Father, who knows and sees all. I don't.

The Lord surprised me once by highlighting a Bible verse. Jesus' words in Luke 17:1 (NIV) blew my mind. It says, *"Jesus said to his disciples, 'Things that cause people to stumble are bound to come, but woe to anyone through whom they come.'"* That *"woe"* there is not for the one who sinned, but for the one who *caused* someone to falter. I don't want to be that one. This doesn't excuse sin, but it comforted me to know that even Jesus recognizes that there are sometimes circumstances that lead people to sin. Sometimes it's best to be silent when a brother or sister falters; we don't know why. God does. OMG!

I've noticed, too, in my Christian journey, the Lord has never bombarded me about sin, unlike many sermons I hear. When He does, He points out the sinful issue, talks to me about it, and then He moves on. He doesn't keep reminding me of it. One time, He points it out. Also, the Lord has never taken my side about another's sinful action toward me. If I complain, He never agrees or criticizes the other person. He never exposes people's flaws or puts them down. Never. OMG! Instead, He's *always pointed me to my own shortcomings*, how I could improve in a situation, or how I could follow Him more closely. Thl recall my mother often saying, "You can't go around blaming people." It's true. We can't. OMG!

Jesus Christ Changes Me

Again, I followed my brother Ron, this time to a new church, where he was the youth pastor. I served as Sunday School registrar and enjoyed it. We were moving away from Pentecostalism and focusing more on God's Word, Jesus Christ, and evangelism and discipleship.

My brother later became a pastor and founded Word of Life Bible Fellowship. There, I learned more about Jesus, salvation, Christian foundations, and the practice of evangelism. The teaching was what I needed. I became engaged as I learned the truth about who Jesus is. I discovered why He matters. The pieces were coming together.

I served in the drama ministry here and had a leading role in a play we produced called "The Mirror." The people were blessed and changed through this production. I enjoy theatre and acting.

Winning souls for Jesus Christ is a priority in the Christian faith, I learned. Jesus termed it with His disciples as becoming a "fisher of men." My brother's church emphasized and taught this. We were involved in various outreach programs, such as those led by Greg Laurie, Dr. Bill Bright's Campus Crusade for Christ, and the Four Spiritual Laws ministry, along with street evangelist Jose Perez's Worldwide Evangelistic Ministries. I enjoyed networking with this ministry the most. During the summer months, we traveled with Evangelist Perez to his street outreaches. We had the service outside, grilled food for attendees, packed grocery bags, and offered clothing for attendees to take as needed. We would walk the neighborhood to talk one-on-one with people about Jesus Christ. It was exciting!

Evangelist Perez had a unique, powerful testimony about his salvation that resonated with his culture. He authored a book titled "I Lived to Tell About It." Evangelist Perez is Hispanic, and most of the evangelistic outreaches took place in Hispanic neighborhoods. With much fervor and in the power of the Spirit, Evangelist Perez would share his testimony in Spanish and English from a stage. People always came forward to receive Christ or to receive prayer for their lives after he preached. It was exciting to watch, but being a participant made it even more exciting. I could better understand evangelism and see it in action.

My brother, sister, and I were worship singers for these outreaches. In 1991, Evangelist Perez invited my siblings and me to travel to Puerto Rico with him to share Christ over there. This was also a very memorable experience. I was 29 years old then. I suppose you could say this was a practical time to apply what I was learning in church about evangelism and discipleship to the streets. I learned a lot about evangelism through this connection. Phenomenal!

Discovering Who I Am

After some time, I noticed a disconnect I was experiencing with family members. I had different opinions from theirs, especially regarding spiritual matters. Clearly, nothing had happened between us. No one said or had done anything to hurt me, other than the usual sibling disagreements. (Yes, we argued, disagreed, and fought, and I shot off words with them, too.) This was not that. As I attended their church services or events, I was no longer receiving anything. There was just emptiness now.

I recall attending services at my brother's church, and it was as if nothing was coming in or going out. I no longer felt the surge of excitement or energy I once had. His words were no longer resonating. I kept going, but nothing. Finally, I wrote my letter of resignation to him, and the day I gave it to him, it was as if I was betraying or losing my best friend. I went to the park and just took a walk. I was incredibly sad but instinctively knew I was right. It was time to move on and find myself in God.

Work Life

I began networking with other churches and ministers and visiting other types of churches, such as AME, Methodist, Baptist, Presbyterian, and others. Most times, I served in an administrative capacity. This was the line of work I did for a living. It's the industry I loved working in and was good at.

A few years after high school, I learned about the Opportunities Industrialization Center (OIC), founded by the late Rev. Leon Sullivan. The center is a vocational, educational, and life skills training program designed to prepare young men and women for full-time employment. I enrolled in the free six-month clerk-typist program. Once I finished the training, I started working at a bank in the Tax Department, preparing personal property tax returns as a general bank clerk. (I had never known about personal property taxes.) I learned about it, however, and started building a reputation in this industry.

After that, I worked as an administrative assistant in different industries, including corporate, childcare, healthcare, legal, nonprofit, and schools. I networked with professionals and enhanced my computer, office, organizational, and communication skills. I was excited! I found out what I excelled at.

Of all the offices I worked in, I preferred those that were luxurious, sophisticated, and had advanced technology. My focus shifted to becoming a successful Fortune 500 executive assistant, earning a substantial income. I noticed how the various professionals with whom I worked had high-end offices, the best computers, wore nice professional clothing, and lived in fancy houses or city apartments. This excited me, along with the conversations and money circulating throughout the industry. I had the energy, skills, and smarts to fit in on this level. So, I began visualizing my life at a much higher level. I told myself, "With your smarts, you can make a lot of money and live in one of those elaborate, exclusive high-rise city lofts." This became my goal, what was driving me.

I gained many skills and met some influential people in each of my jobs. I became more professional. I gained a deeper understanding of the industry and its people, and I developed business acumen. I could work an office! I connected with what these professionals, businesses, or departments needed, and I delivered. I worked on their business communications, streamlined office procedures, provided computer help, organized their paperwork, and helped them meet their goals. As an admin, my bosses never had to step into my lane and deal with details; I did that. "Boy, am I good at this," I often thought! My confidence was at an all-time high. Each job had given me more skills to help me reach my ultimate destination as a top-notch corporate executive. My dream was becoming a reality.

My skill set even gained me a reputation in my neighborhood. People came to me for resume preparation and/or to type business correspondence or to prepare funeral programs. I often assisted my dad, too, by typing his business letters, especially when he needed to complain to companies. My dad told me how his dad had a printing business; I was doing some of the same things my grandfather did, but I never met him; he died while I was a little girl. I became the point of reference in the neighborhood because I was that good. I loved it! Becoming successful was my drive and what I was living for. "I have to succeed," I often thought.

Anyway, at the time my son Bryant was born, I was out of work. I worked at a medical center in my community during his conception, and I liked the job. In fact, I had the pregnancy test done there and freaked out when I learned I was pregnant. I don't know if my disappointment had more to do with my own driven pursuits, my upbringing, or my church. Surely, my getting pregnant was not about disappointing God. At the core of my thinking was, "What will the church people think?" It's strange that Christians do things they know are incorrect, disobey God, and then are surprised by the outcomes. This was me when I learned I was pregnant. I went into a funk, became depressed, started making mistakes at work, and lost the job.

I needed a job to secure a pleasant life for Bryant. I was receiving public assistance when he was born and hated it. Later, my sister, Judy, helped me get a job at her daycare center, where I worked as a secretary. As I told you, Judy is my sister, who has worked as a professional early childhood education teacher; she has done this all her life, and the kids learned under her. Judy would say to me, "I don't know how you can be in an office all day," and I would say, "And I don't know how you can work with kids every day." LOL. Differences. Anyway, I took the job and rushed to call DPA (now called DHS) to inform the case worker that I had found a job. I was thrilled, and so was the caseworker.

I also began thinking about the home Bryant and I needed. I was still living with my mom, who was gracious and helpful, and made everything comfortable for us. However, it became a tight living arrangement with her, and she was making significant sacrifices for us. The Lord provided a home when Bryant was four or five years old. I got the house through a homeownership initiative implemented by the mayor. I had to make repairs to the home, live in it for five years, and then I would own it. The Lord provided me with a comfortable home to raise Bryant.

Academia

I needed more money now, with a growing son who had needs for his physical growth and education, as well as a home to maintain. More bills. After searching for a new job, I left the daycare and started working as an administrative assistant at a college in Philadelphia. I was twenty-six years old. Academia would be the industry I was in for the next ten years of my life.

I loved this job because I worked in University Relations, which involved the public relations, publications, and development departments. I have always had an inherent knack for communication, so this atmosphere excited me, and I learned a lot.

My corporate executive dream was still churning inside me, and it was the path I was pursuing.

Sadly, it was a matter of time before I discovered that the department in which I worked would be folding. I ended up working in the Centennial Office at this college, which was set-up specifically to host the events for the 100-year celebration. When it ended, the staff had to seek alternative employment. I searched and found what I thought was an ideal position—one that would get me even closer to the executive level I was seeking. It was a position working in the president's office at a community college. I was eager, so I applied and got the job.

I pictured the president's office in any company as a bustling place where impressive people made important business decisions; it's busy. I thought I would network with top-level officials within this company and outside, learn the ropes, and further advance my skills. Excitedly, I arranged my work suits and arrived early for work on the first day. I was enthusiastic and ready to learn the tricks and trade on this level. To my surprise and dismay, the job disappointed me after only a month.

The work was minimal. The VPs and department heads oversaw all the incoming work in this Office of the President; their admins handled their department's work. All incoming work to the president's office was delegated down to the appropriate VP, even telephone inquiries. I was accustomed to answering questions, finding solutions for people, solving problems, and transcribing and typing documents. This was not the case here. I was very bored. The most important task for which I and the president's assistant were responsible was setting up the monthly board meetings. "What a bummer," I thought. In our sophisticated corporate work clothes, the executive assistant and I spent most of the day goofing off, chatting, or playing games.

Although I was not happy, I planned to stay because I needed the money. However, out of nowhere, I sensed that something was amiss. I felt so uneasy, and I called my brother and told him, "I think they are going to get rid of me." He thought I was being negative, assured me, and told me to remain calm. I didn't because the feeling remained. I started preparing my resume in anticipation.

Sure enough, my feelings were correct. I came in one day, and the president's assistant told me the president wanted to let me go. Although I had the inclination, it still shocked me. I had a superior work ethic, a pleasant attitude, and I performed well in this field, but I had never experienced being fired from a job before. This was a blow to my ego. I was almost 30 years old.

Again, Out of a Job

I returned home devastated and for several days walked around moping and thinking, "How dare he fire me? My supervisors loved me. How could he treat me this way?" Ugh! I spent many days at home doing little, except searching for another job in the want ads and asking others if they knew about any job openings. (LinkedIn, Glassdoor, or ZipRecruiter were not as popular then.)

But nothing was happening. Companies were not responding to the resumes I submitted, and my leads went nowhere. The eeriness bothered me; I felt uncomfortable. I was putting out resumes with nothing returning for months. I mean *nothing*. Things were typically easy and moved fast for me, but not this time. Something was up.

I started experiencing a strange anxiety and finally picked up my Bible, went to my room, and started reading. During one of these sessions, the Holy Spirit meets me there. You know when the Lord is present because it's just as it says when reading about Jesus in the Bible and the response the people had at His presence, His words, His touch. The Holy Spirit's presence is powerful and engulfs your whole being and the atmosphere you're in. He speaks gently but authoritatively, saying something that amazes you and immediately captures your attention. It's not so overwhelming that it scares you, but you recognize that something bigger than you and profound is in your midst.

The Lord Interrupts

The Holy Spirit illuminated two passages of Scripture during this time; they popped off the pages and caught my attention. One was John 15:1-8, about the vine and the branches. Read it, please. After reading it, my thoughts were about humility. You recall me bragging about how good and confident I was in my career and the skills I had. I excelled in many areas; in fact, I was naturally intelligent, outgoing, an excellent communicator, capable of making things happen, a skilled speller and writer, and a quick learner—traits that have defined me throughout my life. I thought about humility because the Lord highlighted that in the Christian life, as the vine, it is Jesus Christ who produces the results. As a branch on the vine, I must stay connected to Him for results.

Up to this point, I had been relying on myself and all the natural skills, talents, and abilities I possessed, and the way I was culturally groomed. Things stopped moving or happening as easily as before. I continued meditating on this scripture. The Lord showed me how confident I was in myself and in what I could do, which is okay, but I was navigating my path in life. I had set the plan for it.

I focused on verse five, which says, *I am the vine; you are the branches. If you remain in me and I in you, you will bear much fruit; apart from me, you can do nothing.* The "*apart from me, you can do nothing*" part stuck out. "Do nothing?" I thought. I was making tremendous progress in my career and toward my professional goals. "I am doing things," I thought to myself.

As the Lord kept me in this learning posture for weeks, He revealed more to me. The fruit-bearing Jesus Christ is talking about here has nothing to do with my personal life goals, accomplishments, or successes. He was talking about bearing fruit for the kingdom of God. It's why He emphasized "remaining in the vine" to produce kingdom fruit or results.

In my natural ability, yes, my skills and abilities were producing remarkable results for me in my career, but not for the Lord's kingdom agenda. The Lord was pulling me closer to Himself, to something more profound. I can't honestly say that since my salvation, I have remained in the vine. First off, this season in my life was the first time the Lord brought this to my attention. Second, I was navigating my Christian life and deciding based on the skills I had developed in my work and how I performed in my work life. My attempts at living the Christian life were not based on being in the vine. I was simply following what I grew up with, what I saw spiritually in others and how they lived, and my natural giftedness.

I relied heavily on my natural abilities to live a Christian life. It's possibly the reason I failed so often. Natural life principles, natural talents, or inherent skills do not work in mastering God's kingdom life. The Holy Spirit revealed to me that this is how I was processing life in Him.

The results I wanted and was living and working for, however, were for me, not for Him. I continued to lament to the Lord about the job loss and the next one I needed to secure to get my career goals back on track. Softly, the Lord whispers to me, "This is not what I want you to do."

As we will discuss further in the next chapter, Author Millard Erickson stated in his book, "Introducing Christian Doctrine," that "The Holy Spirit is a person, not a vague force, as we identify Him in the Upper Room" (Erickson 77). Until that day, I had never thought of the Holy Spirit as a person; I'm sure my brother taught this, but it did not register with me. Sometimes we must wait for the Lord to reveal Himself to us. The Lord identified a misdirection in my thinking and living. This scared me a bit, as I thought, "Well, if this is not what He wants for me, what does He want? Fear came over me; I was in control of my life. This was an intrusion into my plans. I continued reading, however.

The other passage of Scripture the Lord highlighted for me was in Luke 9:23-26 (NIV). It says, *Then he said to them all, Whoever wants to be my disciple must deny themselves and take up their cross daily and follow me. For whoever wants to save their life will lose it, but whoever loses their life for me will save it. What good is it for someone to gain the whole world, and yet lose or forfeit their very self? Whoever is ashamed of me and my words, the Son of Man will be ashamed of them when he comes in his glory and in the glory of the Father and of the holy angels.* OMG! "This is getting too serious," I thought.

My entire being jolted after reading this. I initially bucked at the message. Reading this passage of Scripture frightened me, too. The words were obvious and revealed the condition of my heart. I was venturing toward gaining more money, success, prestige, and a lavish lifestyle and comfort for my son and me. The Holy Spirit let me know in this season of inactivity, as His follower, He wanted me to: (1) deny myself; (2) take up a cross (give up my career goals and plans); and (3) follow where He wants me. This is what a disciple of Jesus Christ must do, it says. And this is the part I was talking about earlier, which I rarely see or hear in the lives of some people who claim to be Christians, followers of Jesus Christ. Some things may have to go when you meet Jesus. What that is will differ from person to person. It will be unique to you in your journey with Jesus Christ.

"OMG!" I thought. "Give up my plan, my path, my goals, God?" God was coming to me through this verse for something, a tradeoff, a transformation. What would I do?

I was terrified! The Lord was not playing any games with me or sugarcoating His words. He did not smooth the words over to make me feel comfortable. The words in these verses of Scripture about what a follower or disciple of Jesus Christ must do are clear as day. The Lord was serious, and I knew it. I never thought life in Christ would get this personal, this deep. OMG!

My life was fine and progressing well for both Bryant and me. I was comfortable with the way things were. *Why is He interrupting things?* I thought. The Lord was calling me to have a deeper relationship with Himself. "Yikes! What am I going to do?"

This season in my life is what I believe was my personal "fisher of men" call. It happened when life disappointed me, things stopped moving as usual, and I had time to slow down, sit, think, and listen. It may not happen in the same way for you.

I pondered the Lord's revelations to me, first about where my heart was and what was driving it. I believe, first, the Lord must reveal the condition of our hearts to determine whether they align with His. Usually, ours is not because the heart is "desperately wicked," as we learn in Jeremiah 17:9. Next, He wants to see if we're willing to make the trade; He asks for something—a surrender, a giving up of ourselves, our desires, and our pursuits for His.

So many things ran through my mind. I was pacing the floor contemplating this, and I became afraid. I wondered, "What is He going to do with me, my life?" Although there was no need for my apprehension, the Lord did not scold me for it.

The Holy Spirit intervened in my life, prompting me to surrender it to Him. I was content with my life and had fallen into a comfortable pattern. Things were progressing for me. My nine-to-five work schedule was convenient. I'd finish work, come home to do homework with Bryant, cook dinner, eat with him, then go back out the door again to an outdoor activity or another church or family event. This routine worked fine for me, so I didn't like what God was asking of me.

Last, God showed me one last thing that put the icing on the cake. As I walked around my community more often now that I was out of work, I took notice of the environment in which I lived. I had been aloof to it and the neighbors. I had little interaction with them, apart from my son's friends and the business I handled for some. I hadn't visited their homes or attended any of their social activities. I talked little to them. In fact, the people and neighborhood weren't on my radar. With my consistent schedule, I wasn't paying much attention to what was happening in my neighborhood or with the surrounding people.

The Lord opened my eyes, and my heart became sensitized. Some residents sat on the steps all day, looking somber and unmotivated. Others stood on the corners every day chatting with each other, drinking a beer, and never going to work. I saw some guys just nodding off from taking some type of drug. Many of the young ladies had drug dependencies and were involved with men who supported their habits.

I paid more attention to the people who came to me for typing services. I was casually perusing their documents and rushed to complete them just to collect the extra money. A closer look showed me that their writing and spelling were terrible. They lacked basic educational skills; they were illiterate. That's why they were coming to me. All this time, I was only doing this work as a side hustle, but a need was there. I could not believe it! My heart ached, and a profound sadness welled up within me. Wow!

Upon talking to my neighbors, I learned many were relying on drugs or alcohol. One lady told me she was very depressed and had never taken the bus to downtown Philadelphia. Wow! I felt horrified that I had not noticed these things. Another woman said to me, "Ellie, I wish I could dress like you and go to work like that every day." OMG! My heart sank. I melted at her words. I felt ashamed because they saw me, but I didn't see them.

My life and focus had been all about me and my own interests. I was self-absorbed, self-focused, and self-driven. The Holy Spirit, however, knew; it's why He interrupted—disrupting my comfort zone, breaking my heart, and making me cry — to give me a "fisher of men" eyes and heart; something only He can do.

The Lord's intervention during this season of my life changed it from a "me" focus existence to a Christ-focused one. That's the pivotal point of fishing for Him. You accept what He reveals about yourself that needs to be changed and then receive His renewing grace to begin to see and feel as He does for others, to love them as He does. Change can never happen until you first accept the truth about what you are not. Only with this renewed heart and mind can we be effective fishers of men and serve people with His eyes and heart.

After some time, I finally said, "Okay. Yes, Lord, I surrender to Your will for me." I felt a release and freedom in saying it, but I did not know all it meant. It didn't matter then.

Interestingly, a few things happened shortly thereafter. First, I recognized that the executive assistant level I had so desperately aspired to reach did not even align with my personality. I really do enjoy helping people, finding solutions for them, and teaching them how to do something. I enjoy being in the thick of things. Twiddling my fingers all day at work was not exciting and didn't challenge my mind. I enjoy producing results.

I started chatting regularly with the woman who told me she had never been to downtown Philadelphia. I learned more about her life. We developed a relationship in which she would visit my home, or I would visit hers. I learned she was a lifelong substance user and suffered from severe depression. She asked to study the Bible with me. We met at her home or mine weekly for one hour. Learning about the Bible and knowing the Lord thrilled her! The study eventually expanded to include her entire family: her husband, two daughters, and son. They all accepted Christ's message of salvation, and their family changed quickly before my eyes; I was amazed! Her family's entire disposition changed; her children were now so happy to see their mom's transition. She became drug-free. Later, she moved from Philadelphia to the countryside in upstate Pennsylvania. The last I heard, she was doing well and happy. I discovered that I also enjoy teaching the Bible.

I also later responded to the drug-dependent woman who said she wished she could dress like me and go to work. I told her, "You can go to work like me!" It was honest. I honestly believed she could and would show her how.

This is the "why" of becoming a fisher of men—to catch people and bring them to God. We're all different, and our relationship with the Lord is personal to us. This is the way the Lord called me to be a fisher of men. For you, the circumstances in which He may transform your heart may be quite different. He knows us completely and meets each of us in unique ways. God may call people to Himself or change their hearts in various ways; we cannot restrict ourselves to a single, systematic approach. We do not know and can't comprehend how the Spirit of God may flow; we must allow Him to have free course.

The miracle of the large catch of fish Jesus performed with the disciples is an interesting story. Please read it in Luke 5:1-11. (I love the way the series The Chosen depicts it.) Unbeknownst to the disciples, this miracle was not just to settle their debts or to show Jesus' power. It was also to drive home Jesus' lesson to them about catching men; they probably didn't recognize it at that moment, but as they started making disciples, there's no doubt in my mind that they recalled this miracle of the large catch of fish. We need to bring this heart of Christ's ministry back to the forefront in the Church.

Finally, a New Job!

I was out of work for a few more months. After a lot of prayer and many interviews at prestigious companies, the next job I landed and stayed in for five years was not the one I wanted or anything typical of what I liked in an office. The office was dusty and disorganized. The computers, office furniture, desks, and equipment were old and outdated; the installed computer system was Winstar. OMG! The office was not an office at all; it was a mess. It did not appeal to me. I left the interview and returned home, and once again I accurately discerned things. I said to myself, "That's the job you're going to get." And I did.

But, boy, did the Lord shine on me in this job, and I made some profound discoveries about myself. I worked harder than I ever had, served more young people than ever, and transformed that office into a place where faculty members could easily locate things and follow the processes I put in place. They could now be who they were—professors. This became my work philosophy from that day on in my career. Amazing!

This season in my life remains with me; the verses of Scripture are paramount in my mind today. The Lord has ordered my life so much so that now I know I must depend entirely on Him and His guidance to get it right or accomplish anything for His kingdom; otherwise, it doesn't work.

Today, I'm more conscious of my pursuits and endeavors, and I bring everything before the Lord before I do or join in anything. I'm more discerning about who comes into my life and wants to connect with me to take part in things or use my multiple gifts. I want nothing to derail me from God's mission for me, throw me off course, or cause me to wither and die apart from the vine. I had to keep the lessons from that season in my mind and in my heart. This too needs to be brought back to the forefront of the Church of Jesus Christ.

Would you believe that, with all the colleges I worked for, I could have gotten a free degree? But I didn't get my bachelor's degree until 2018. Silly girl! This is what I mean about being unwise, misdirected, and a procrastinator. Don't be like me in this, younger gen. Follow Jesus! *Make the most of every opportunity...* (Ephesians 5:16 NLT)

Chapter 10 - How Jesus Christ Speaks Today and How Will I Know?

But the Helper, the Holy Spirit, whom the Father will send in my name will teach you all things and bring to your remembrance all that I have said to you. (John 14:26 ESV)

Throughout this book, you've often heard me mention the Holy Spirit, especially in the previous chapter. My experiences—of hearing the Lord speak to me, being guided by Him, and becoming attuned to the needs of others—all raise the question at the heart of this chapter: How is God speaking today, and how can we discern if it is truly Him speaking to us?

As I shared in Chapter 4, Hebrews 1:1-2 (NIV) says: *"In the past God spoke to our ancestors through the prophets at many times and in various ways. But in these last days he has spoken to us by his Son, whom he appointed heir of all things, and through whom also he made the universe."*

So, in times past, God spoke through the prophets, then He spoke by sending Jesus Christ, as a man, to show us what He is like. The main point I emphasize in this chapter is how Jesus Christ continues to speak to us—now through the Holy Spirit. The Holy Spirit is continuing Jesus' mission and reinforcing what He said and did. If you're reading the Bible for the first time, this may be a new concept, but please stay with me as we explore how Jesus' voice remains active through the Holy Spirit.

You may ask: Who is the Holy Spirit? How is He connected to Jesus Christ? What is His role in the life of believers and nonbelievers, and in the Church? Is His presence visible or audible? Several sources will help clarify these and other questions about the Holy Spirit in this chapter. Follow along.

The Holy Spirit is the third person of the Godhead (aka the Trinity), which includes God the Father, God the Son, and God the Holy Spirit. We established earlier that I (and perhaps many of you) failed to recognize Him as such. All three are God, who exists and reveals Himself in three different persons. This too may sound somewhat unusual. Throughout history, many philosophers and religious scholars have offered important ideas about the Trinity. Although various controversies also ensued about Him, with Scripture and in time, one can grasp this nature of the Godhead.

First, it's essential that we understand that there is no inequality in the Godhead. The Father, Son, and Holy Spirit are all God and coequal. Each operates with distinct characteristics but shares a common relational goal with humankind.

In most of this book, I emphasized God the Son, Jesus Christ. We discussed how God manifested Himself through Jesus Christ, who came down in the flesh to live among humanity, demonstrating to us what God is like and completing God's mission to save and bring humanity to God. Jesus accomplished this without corruption. He ascended back to God after finishing his work on earth and promised to send the Holy Spirit to his disciples (John 14:16).

When examining the distinct characteristics of the Holy Spirit, we should know that He operates toward the same goal as God the Father and God the Son. Specifically, Jesus Christ told His followers that the Holy Spirit would be the One continuing His mission after He left the earth. Because the Holy Spirit now speaks, teaches, guides, and supports them, they must follow Him in order to continue Jesus Christ's work (John 14:15-31).

Jesus and the Holy Spirit were always in intimate fellowship with each other. The Spirit was always with Jesus, from His birth to His resurrection, and assisting Him in all He was and did. He relied on the Holy Spirit, availed of His power, and respected His role throughout His earthly journey.

Jesus also spoke about the Holy Spirit with His disciples, telling them who He was, what He would do, and their need for Him. How many times did Jesus speak about the Holy Spirit? "Around 93 times, the reference is to the Holy Spirit in the Bible..." (Wikipedia, The Free Encyclopedia).

The infographic below lists verses of Scripture that mention Jesus with the Holy Spirit or where Jesus speaks about the Holy Spirit. For clarity, read the surrounding scriptures. Then, for context and understanding, read the entire chapter where the Scripture is located.

The Holy Spirit and Jesus

OLD TESTAMENT	
Isaiah 11:2; 42:1; 61:1	The Holy Spirit is prophesied that He would be on Jesus when He comes
NEW TESTAMENT	
Matthew 1:18, 20; Luke 1:35	Jesus is conceived by the Holy Spirit
Matthew 3:11; Mark 1:8; Luke 3:16; John 1:33	John the Baptist says Jesus will baptize with the Holy Spirit.
Matthew 3:16-17; Mark 1:10; Luke 3:21-22; John 1:32-33	Holy Spirit descends on Jesus in bodily form at his baptism; Spirit of God descends on Jesus like a dove at his baptism by John.
Matthew 4:1; Mark 1:12; Luke 4:1-2	Jesus, filled with the Holy Spirit, was led into the wilderness and tempted for 40 days.
Matthew.10:19-20; Mark 13:11; Luke 12:12:	The Holy Spirit will teach what you should say during persecution.; Spirit of your father will be speaking through them.
Isaiah 42:1; Matthew 12:18; Acts 1:16; 4:25	Reference to David speaking by the Holy Spirit, quote from Isaiah, the chosen servant, spirit on him.
Matthew 12:28; Luke 11:20	If I cast out demons by the Spirit of God.
Matthew 12:31-32; Mark 3:29; Luke 12:10	Blasphemy against the Holy Spirit is not forgiven.
Luke 1:13-15	Angel to Zechariah, John child will be filled with the Holy Spirit.
Luke 1:35	Angel to Mary announcing Jesus' conception, the Holy Spirit will come upon you.
Luke 1:41-42	Elizabeth filled with the Holy Spirit at Mary's visit

Learn about the Holy Spirit

Since Christ speaks now through the Holy Spirit, we must learn about Him. Author Millard J. Erickson supports the importance of learning about the Holy Spirit. He states, "A second reason the study of the Holy Spirit is especially important is that we live in a period in which the Holy Spirit's work is prominent than that of the other members of the Trinity... If we are to be in touch with God today, we must become acquainted with the Holy Spirit's activity" (Erickson 270-271). This is paramount for Christians to realize. The Holy Spirit now performs the work of Jesus Christ—informing us, recalling His words, and directing us. Yes, Jesus Christ has finished His earthly work and ascended back to the Father, but He is still alive. His mission and work continue.

Many experts on the Bible agree that people often misuse or misunderstand the Holy Spirit. Theologian Alister E. McGrath observes that because "theological discussions were focused on other topics, the Holy Spirit wasn't widely discussed in the first three centuries. The debate ensued over whether the Holy Spirit should be treated as an activity, as creator, or as God," (McGrath 227-228). Today, people still seem to debate how they should identify or appropriate the Holy Spirit. The understanding of who the Holy Spirit is and how He functions varies among different church denominations. This should not be in the universal Church.

A Gift to Us

Alister McGrath also helps us know that the Holy Spirit is a gift. He writes, "The Holy Spirit is a gift to believers, given by the Father God, who continues the work of Jesus Christ in their lives and the church. The Holy Spirit's name in Hebrew is ruach, and in Greek, pneuma, meaning 'breath' or 'wind,' which is translated as 'spirit,' denoting an unseen, life-giving force. United with holy,' the force is said to be divine, though the combination of the two words occurs only three times in the OT: (Isa. 63:10,11; Ps. 51:11)" (McGrath 227-228).

McGrath also notes, "In addition, doctrinal truths on His character and role are developed in the New Testament letters. 'Augustine regards the Spirit as the bond of unity between the Father and Son, on the one hand, and between God and believers, on the other. The Spirit unites believers both to God and to other believers, upon which the unity of the church ultimately depends" (McGrath 231).

Notice the keywords here: "unity of the church." Christ's Church was never meant to think or act apart from other believers. This is a cause of so many divisions today.

McGrath concludes:

> It is evident from Scripture who the Holy Spirit is and how He functions. His attributes and activity are highlighted in the book of Acts. In addition, doctrinal truths about His character, work, and function are developed in the New Testament letters. Those who may have difficulty in surrendering control of their lives to the Holy Spirit because they do not identify Him as a coequal with God the Father and God the Son are most likely the ones who find it difficult to define and/or understand who He is. Others have never been accurately taught about Him as part of the Godhead, or as deity (McGrath 231).

This is awesome teaching!

The Holy Spirit as a Person

In his book, *Introducing Christian Doctrine*, Millard Erickson helps us identify the Holy Spirit as a person. He writes, "The Holy Spirit is a person, not a vague force, as we identify Him in the Upper Room... Most of us may recall the Holy Spirit's first appearance to the disciples in the book of Acts, where He appeared as a mighty rushing wind and filled them. Instead, the Holy Spirit is a gift to believers, given by God the Father. He continues the work of Jesus Christ, who ascended back to the Father after he died on earth... The work of the Spirit is not completed when one becomes a believer; it is just the beginning" (Erickson).

The Holy Spirit is Powerful

Author and Theologian, Walter Elwell also helps us understand the Holy Spirit. He writes in "The Evangelical Dictionary of Theology":

> Jesus, as the God-Man, demonstrated both the intrinsic and derived aspects of power. He proclaimed his power and authority as derived from the Father (John 5:27; 17:2; 5:16-23). He also demonstrated that his power was derived from his authority as the Son of Man and that the two were an inseparable testimony to his divine nature" (Matt. 9:6-7; Luke 4:36; 9:1)... He continues how, "Power in the New Testament is used to

describe the unseen world. The angelic realm is described as "powers" or "authorities" (Rom. 8:38; Eph 3:10; 6:12; Col 1:16; 2:10; 2:16). Jesus exercised power over the unseen world through his exorcism of demons (Mark 6:7; Luke 9:1) (Elwell).

The most amazing thing I read is the Apostle Paul's claim in Romans 8:11 and Ephesians 1:19-20. He states that the power that resurrected Jesus (related to salvation) is the same power that is in believers and the Church today. Wow!

The Holy Spirit's Work to Change Us

Christ always did what pleased the Father (John 8:29), so the Holy Spirit brings us to a proper understanding of God's word to transform us into Christ's image. This was a struggle for me, and it took me a while to learn. Maybe it's a struggle for you, too. Misrepresentations of the Holy Spirit multiply because of ignorance or pride. People have said words to me that God was supposed to have said. Things He was telling me to do through another person. Healing will take place through the Holy Spirit if I do a particular thing. Or a preacher rebuked the congregation in church, warning them about a specific sin. These actions can lead to embarrassing situations, hurt feelings, or cause someone to stumble in their faith. It's a confusing 'OMG' moment, especially when the spoken words don't happen.

I've experienced the challenge of trying to live like Christ, even after listening to the Holy Spirit or reading the Bible, just as you may have. Painfully so, there were many peaks and valleys, as well as trials. My head was spinning, as if on a merry-go-round or roller coaster ride. Or I was on this treadmill way of living, speeding up for a minute, then slowing down to catch my breath when I got tired. You never get off it because it's all you know—STRIVE. It works, you think, so you remain on it for a long time.

This is not the Holy Spirit's doing. Striving, trying, pushing, endeavoring to get it right! The Holy Spirit does not lead us to get on a treadmill to strengthen our biceps, triceps, or any other "ceps." He's not pushing us like our friends do when we're overweight. In fact, Jesus Christ eliminated the entire treadmill process from the Christian experience. He never intended it to be this way. "Treadmill thinking" stems from cultural pressures, external influences, social comparisons, and the examples set by religious figures. My sisters are a case in point. They were more mature, disciplined, and devoted to God, so they avoided some things that I didn't; I tried my best to be like them. There is, however, only one model in the Christian faith—Jesus Christ. He began our faith and will finish it. He's the only icon to be like.

It wasn't until many years into my Christian journey did the Holy Spirit lighten this load and relieve me of this treadmill way of thinking. He clarified a Scripture passage for me in Galatians 5:16 (NIV), which says, *So I say, walk by the Spirit, and you will not gratify the desires of the flesh.* OMG!

I was striving to remove my sinful tendencies and change my negative personality traits as I saw fit or as others suggested I should. But I continuously repeated them, though. What this wonderful verse of Scripture says to me (in plain language) is, "If the Holy Spirit says turn left, and I turn left, I win in being like Christ. If the Holy Spirit says turn left, but I turn right, I lose at conforming to Christ. If He says "stop," and I stop, I win. If He says "go," and I go, I win. Are you getting the picture? This is profoundly simple and not cumbersome.

Therefore, we need to understand the Holy Spirit's roles, how He operates, and what He teaches. It's essential to listen to and obey His guidance. This is God speaking to us through the Holy Spirit. We change and grow to be like Christ this way. Scripture reveals in Romans 8:29 how it was God's predetermined will (decided on in advance) to transform us to be like *Christ*, not the bishop, the pastor, the first lady, the deacons, our family members, or another "good" church member. If we understood this about the Holy Spirit, we would not need to spend so much time and energy trying to fix our sinful tendencies or the sins of others. We can't! It's the Holy Spirit's work! Remember our discussion about how Jesus told His disciples, "I will make you?" Aaaah!

The Holy Spirit as Illuminator

As we read the Bible, the Holy Spirit will guide us in its interpretation. He helps us understand what the Scriptures are saying. He illuminates or shines a light on scripture. Founder R. C. Sproul writes:

> Divine illumination and the internal testimony of the Holy Spirit are closely related. In both cases, the Spirit works in and through the inscripturated words of God's prophets and Apostles. When it comes to divine illumination, however, we are speaking more about the Holy Spirit's work to give us understanding of Scripture than we are talking about the Spirit's confirmation that we are God's children. Sometimes in our lives when we are reading the Bible, suddenly we are struck by something in the text that we have never

noticed before. Perhaps we suddenly see how the passage applies to our specific context. Maybe we understand the contours of an argument that escaped us previously. These are examples of the Holy Spirit's work of illumination (Sproul, Divine Illumination).

This reminds me of when I told you I was out of a job, and the Holy Spirit illuminated John 15 and Luke 9 for me. Those Scriptures stuck out in that season of my life because the Lord was about to transform me. This is the way Christ speaks today—through the Holy Spirit, and He always aligns with the scriptures.

The Apostle Paul in 1 Corinthians 2:6-16 describes the work of illumination.

The Holy Spirit as Comforter

With all the "breaking news" in our day (and there's a lot of it that breaks our heart), we need someone with whom we can share the blows, comfort the pain we feel, and share the experience. The Holy Spirit does this.

John 14 begins with Jesus having a conversation with His disciples about not being troubled by anything in life. His Father's house has many rooms, which Jesus is preparing for us to inhabit one day. He was also preparing them for His soon-to-be departure from this life, although they did not immediately realize this. When we come to verse 16 (NIV), Jesus says, A*nd I will ask the Father, and he will give you another advocate to help you and be with you forever — the Spirit of truth. The world cannot accept him because it neither sees him nor knows him. But you know him, for he lives with you and will be with you.* The ESV version uses the word "helper." The KJV uses the word "comforter," and the CSB version uses the word "counselor." These are all correct identities of the Holy Spirit, and I've experienced Him in each of these ways. The Holy Spirit is an advocate, helper, comforter, and counselor.

This means that in our Christian journey, we can rely on the Holy Spirit to gently advocate for us when declaring the truth about Christ or when we face persecution. He will also help us when we are weak, tempted, or stressed. When I hear the term comforter, gentleness comes to my mind. We can count on the Holy Spirit's comfort when we are sad, experience loss, or are intimidated, bullied, or put down. Last, we don't always know what the best decision is. The Holy Spirit will counsel us when tough decisions need to be made or provide clarity on the direction we should take. He will also teach us all things.

I laughed at one comedian I heard make a joke about God's guidance. He said, "You got people talking about asking the Lord for help to find a parking space. I mean, a parking space, come on." The Holy Spirit sure does help with that. My sister, with whom I often rode, always prayed for help to find a parking space, and the Holy Spirit helped her find one. LOL.

Overall, He is a faithful friend. I am a witness that the Holy Spirit does all of this and more.

The Holy Spirit's Power for Our Witnessing

Finally, one role of the Holy Spirit that many of us really overlook or don't know about is the Holy Spirit's transforming work that makes us magnets for drawing people into God's kingdom. Our qualities, personality, knowledge, and attitudes are interesting, and people want to know who Jesus Christ is. Or, we have a zeal, a passion to share Jesus Christ with others. Is this what is happening in some of our churches today? It appears we're turning many away rather than drawing them to God. OMG!

Jesus said the Holy Spirit would fill us with His power, but for what reason? Acts 1:8 (ESV) tells us, *But you will receive power when the Holy Spirit has come upon you, and you* ***will be my witnesses****...* Jesus told His disciples they would receive the Holy Spirit's power to share the testimony of Jesus Christ with others. (And, boy, did they!) We have disregarded this aspect of the Holy Spirit's power source. OMG!

We often think the Holy Spirit's power is limited to emotional displays such as dancing, speaking in tongues, singing, making melodious music, praying for healing, giving prophecies, or seeking blessings. Please understand me here; there are times when the Holy Spirit does come in the atmosphere and touches us as a "mighty rushing wind." He is so powerful that He releases a fervent reaction in us, where we may jump and dance, clap our hands, cry, or sing and play our instruments melodiously, as never before. However, this is not the primary reason for having the Holy Spirit.

The Holy Spirit's dunamis power (from which we derive our English words "dynamic" or "dynamite") manifests in us, providing us the ability, strength, and enablement to boldly witness to others about God's amazing, saving grace through Jesus Christ. His power strengthens us to share with others how He saved you and can save them, too. This is the power of the Holy Spirit that the Lord is talking about, which He fills us with. Pay it forward; tell somebody.

This is what I want to discuss in the sequel to this book.

A Time I Failed to Obey the Holy Spirit

I was about 34-35 years old and worked for a university in a department of about sixteen faculty members. There was an esteemed professor who had an excellent reputation among colleagues worldwide and among the other professors on staff. He was born in another country, not America. The Lord clearly spoke to me one day to share the gospel with him (to tell him about Jesus). I said I would but didn't at that moment. Several days passed by, and the Holy Spirit spoke to me again, "Tell [so and so] about me." This time, I paid closer attention and made a mental note to talk with him. Again, it slipped my mind, and I never followed through. A third time, the Holy Spirit speaks to me again, "Get the gospel to [so and so]."

I remembered on a day the professor had come into the office, and I made plans with him to have lunch. He appeared to be intoxicated. In fact, he had been coming into the department often, smelling of alcohol and staggering a bit. Nonetheless, I called him over and said, "[So and so], let's do lunch one day." He happily agreed, and we set a date. The day was drawing near for our lunch date, but I never followed up or called his home to remind him of our appointment. It was not a priority in my mind. To be honest, when the Lord first spoke to me, his educational background and intellectual status somewhat intimidated me. "Me share Jesus with him?" I thought. "I'm only an admin assistant here. " I frequently experience fear or intimidation when the Lord asks me to do something. The professor and I never made it to lunch.

Several weeks passed. I went into my second office when I had work to do for the graduate program. With the door open, I was working at my desk. One of the other professors peeked in and stood in the doorway. He said to me in what seemed like a penetrating tone, "Oh, I want to let you know, [so and so] died today." It was the professor God told me to share the gospel with.

My heart dropped, and it felt like the most ferocious gut punch hit me in my stomach. I gasped for breath. I was stunned, hurt, surprised, and devastated. I closed the door and cried. With tears flowing and in a whimpering voice, I called my brother. He was compassionate and consoled me but emphasized the importance of obeying the Holy Spirit's leading.

This is another way the Holy Spirit may speak to us about those who may need or are ready to hear the gospel message. He impresses a person in your mind, puts them in your spirit, or speaks directly to you about what to do or say to them, as He did to me. I still think about that experience and how the Lord knew he was nearing the end of his life; the Lord cared for him. He was counting on me to share Jesus Christ with him, but I blew it. Days after, I kept saying, "Lord, I hope you sent someone else along to talk to him about You." No, that wasn't the lesson. I was the one the Lord was counting on to do this. He commissioned me at that moment to share Jesus' message with that professor because He knew He was about to die. The Lord knows what is going on in a person's life and why He commissions us to say certain words to them.

Following this, I pledged to God that I would share my faith whenever He wanted, no matter my fears, a person's status, their race, their intelligence, or the context. To this day, I do. I don't hesitate when I hear the Lord say, "Go."

Confusion about the Holy Spirit

We must teach and bring back to the forefront the Holy Spirit and His role in the life of Christians and the Church. Our failure to understand His equality with God, the lack of teaching about Him, and our own wrong ideas about the Holy Spirit prevent us from recognizing how He is speaking to us today.

I reiterate that the Holy Spirit is continuing Jesus' mission. He is reminding us of, or reinforcing, the same message that Jesus proclaimed. Walter Kaiser writes, "The Spirit's ministry is understood as a continuation and elaboration of that of the Son; He will bring to remembrance what He said (John 14:26); He will bear witness to the Son (John 15:26); and He will declare what He hears from the Son, [thus glorifying] Him (John 16:13-14)" (Kaiser). Kaiser also insists that "theology must be objectively (of a person or their judgment) not influenced by personal feelings or opinions in considering and representing facts derived from the text; it is not to be subjectively imposed on the text by the interpreter... the Spirit of God is the teacher (John 14:16; 16:5-15; 1 John 2:27) and the source of truth and power for effective Bible teaching" (Kaiser).

We must accept what the Bible has said about who the Holy Spirit is and how He functions, and add nothing to it. It is not possible for us to determine this. We should not argue with others about how the Holy Spirit functions based on the varied practices within our church denominations. As we noted earlier, God is impartial. As such, we can conclude that the Holy Spirit has no favorite church denomination; as H We must rid ourselves of personal feelings, biases, or opinions about the Holy Spirit and stick with what Scripture says about Him. Jesus Christ always availed Himself of the Holy Spirit's presence, and He taught and showed us how His ministry works.

I've listened to some of the controversy surrounding the Holy Spirit and heard various opinions about how He works. Most times, the controversy or debate centers around a person's church affiliation or denomination. I know this is true because leaders or members of specific churches have prevented me from saying or doing things, claiming it's not done that way in their church; there was a proper protocol I had to follow. I've also been told I needed the Holy Spirit when I knew I had Him already.

Some individuals failed to recognize Him in my life because I lacked what their church denomination believes is evidence of having the Holy Spirit. Personally, I believe this is why Jesus Christ never intended for God's Church to be divided by denomination; it's One Church. How we see the Holy Spirit is frequently shaped by our loyalty to a church affiliation or long-held religious traditions, not by the Bible. These determine how we perceive the Holy Spirit, and this is not good and is a cause of trouble.

There are historical roots to explain how denominations came to be. The website GotQuestions.org has an article that answers the question "Why Are There So Many Christian Denominations?" They write:

> To answer this question, we must first differentiate between denominations within the body of Christ and non-Christian cults and other religions. Presbyterians and Lutherans are examples of Christian denominations. Mormons and Jehovah's Witnesses are examples of cults (groups claiming to be Christian but denying one or more of the essentials of the Christian faith). Islam and Buddhism are entirely separate religions... The rise of denominations within the Christian faith can be traced back to the Protestant Reformation, the movement to "reform" the Roman Catholic Church during the 16th century, out of which four major divisions or traditions of Protestantism would emerge: Lutheran, Reformed, Anabaptist, and Anglican. From these four, other denominations grew over the centuries.... There seem to be at least two major problems with denominationalism. First, nowhere in Scripture is there a mandate for denominationalism; to the contrary, the mandate is for union and connectivity. Thus, the second problem is that history tells us that denominationalism is the result of, or caused by, conflict and confrontation, which leads to division and separation" (GotQuestions Ministries).

So, we can see that denominations in the Church arose from people's opinions and are not mandated in Scripture. GotQuestions.org agrees that denominations do not promote unity, as Jesus suggested the Church of Christ should.

Remember, too, that the Holy Spirit is described as being like the wind. I don't know about you, but I've watched them on television and have endured windstorms; they freely swirl around, fast, and uncontrollably, affecting the area where they are, moving things around. Wind is mighty and cannot be contained. This suggests to me that the Holy Spirit wants to have free course to flow among us, in our lives, and in our church services. Unfortunately, I have observed how the Holy Spirit is at work in different church denominations, and many times His Spirit *is not flowing freely, if at all.* We've put the brakes on Him. I told you I grew up in the Pentecostal denomination and loved its emotional excitement and fervor. Pentecostal, Holiness, COGIC, and Word of Faith denominations often seem to emphasize the Holy Spirit, but sometimes inappropriately.

Catholicism seems to support the importance of the sacraments in experiencing God's presence. Other movements, such as Protestant (Baptist, Methodist, Lutheran, AME, Presbyterian, Episcopal, etc.), appear to suppress or not fully embrace the Holy Spirit's activity. I've taken part in some of these services. Most of the time, Sunday or weekly services and spiritual programs are rigid. The order of service is set and must not be altered, even if the Holy Spirit desires a change. It seems they cannot detract from its practices. Sometimes, the concern seems to be about what the congregation will think; ministers do not want to offend them or keep them too long. It seems there's some worry or fear about letting the Holy Spirit direct our services, sermons, and activities. Elders have the strongest voices. Committees are in charge. Trustees control the finances. This is not a criticism of anyone's church, but my own observations from attending or serving in several. Again, God established one Church, which was to be unified.

Analogy from a Writer's Perspective

In college, they teach in writing courses that you must first state the central claim you want to discuss in a paper. Then, you are to choose and state subclaims or points about the central claim you wish to discuss in more detail. Instructors also advise you to gather evidence that will support your claim. You can't just provide your own thoughts on a topic; you won't seem credible. To be taken as genuine and credible, you need backup. Find someone who is reliable and already credible, who supports your ideas or perspective. Use those people's words and mix them with yours by quoting, paraphrasing, or summarizing that source's words. Never, ever change them, however. This way helps you look more credible, supports the claim you're making, and gives people a greater reason to believe you. Your evidence won't back up your argument if you stray from your main idea. It will not make any sense or agree at all. The writing is now flawed, distorted, confusing, and lacks synthesis. You must stay on track with your central claim.

Think of the Holy Spirit in this analogy. The Holy Spirit is a credible source for Jesus Christ. He was sent to advocate only for Jesus Christ, to reveal His ways, uphold His message to the world, and guide us in fulfilling His mission.

When we spread ideas that Jesus didn't share or show, the Holy Spirit will not act as a reliable source for our inaccurate message. The Holy Spirit is not making accurate, contrived, supposed "prophetic words" we spoke to people. Also, when we speak over the Holy Spirit or in His place, we distort His message and confuse people. The Holy Spirit cares about people. We shouldn't use the Holy Spirit to trick, frighten, or pressure people, because this can cause pain and confusion, and make them turn away from God.

Questions for Thought

We've covered a lot about the Holy Spirit—who He is, how He works and guides us, and how Jesus proclaimed Him and availed Himself of His work. This spawns some questions for us to consider.

- Do we really believe that the Holy Spirit, too, is God, who sees all, knows all, and is still building Christ's Church?
- If Jesus, the Christ, recognized, followed, listened to, depended on, and availed Himself of the Holy Spirit's work in His ministry, who are we that we do not? Jesus always knew what to teach, what to say to others, when to perform a healing or miracle, the mood of a place, people's hearts and thoughts, and when to go alone to pray.
- Is it possible that in Christendom today, we have forgotten about the significant role the Holy Spirit plays in a believer's life and the Church? Do we think Jesus' death finished it all?
- Have we eliminated the Holy Spirit's work altogether? Our attitude now is, "We've got this." "We're in control of everything."
- With all the advancements we've made in politics, society, education, science, and

technology, do we still require the Holy Spirit's help? Do we trust in and rely on these advancements *more* than we do on the Holy Spirit?

- Have earthly comforts dimmed our eyes, clogged our ears, or desensitized our hearts?
- Have we attempted to blend the methods this world employs with the workings of the Holy Spirit?
- Are the Holy Spirit's ways of working extreme or mysterious to us now, so we're ashamed and afraid to let Him have His way?
- Have we grieved the Holy Spirit, where He's sad and has taken a back seat? Scripture tells us to, *Grieve not the Holy Spirit* (Eph. 4:30 KJV).
- Do you think maybe the Holy Spirit is not flowing as mightily in and through us as before because He recognizes where He is no longer wanted or needed and has stepped back and let us have our way?
- Do we deny or reject His help, or have we opted for a new way instead of Jesus Christ's way?
- Has the promised Spirit of Truth stopped talking because your message is no longer about Jesus Christ but about gaining notoriety, being politically correct, not being offensive, becoming popular, entertaining, or performance-driven?
- Since the Holy Spirit's job is to represent Jesus, but Christians have pushed Him aside, whose spirit is influencing us? Whose power are we operating in?
- Have we neglected to do the one thing the Holy Spirit asked us to do a week, a month, or years ago? We've short circuited Him. (We sure cannot judge the Israelites' 40-year journey through the wilderness; we are just like them.)

We pray as David prayed in Psalm 51:10-12 (NASB 1995), *Create in me a clean heart, O God, and renew a steadfast spirit within me. Do not cast me away from Your presence. And do not take Your Holy Spirit from me. Restore to me the joy of Your salvation, and sustain me with a willing spirit…*

ROLES OF THE HOLY SPIRIT

The Holy Spirit is powerful (like the wind)
(Luke 4:14; John 3:8; Acts 1:8, 2:1-4; Romans 15:19)

The Holy Spirit is a promised gift, sent by Jesus after He left the earth. He can be asked for.
(Luke 24:49; *John 14:26-27; Acts 1:4, 2:38)*

The Holy Spirit dwells in believers and fills them. He can be known.
(John 7:37-39, 14:17; 1 Corinthians 3:16)

The Holy Spirit is a source of God's Revelation, Wisdom, and Power
(1 Corinthians 2:10-11)

The Holy Spirit is the Spirit of Truth, who is wise and illuminates Scripture.
(1 Corinthians 2:10-13; Ephesians 1:17-18; John 14:26 and 16:13)

The Holy Spirit is the Spirit Truth, who guides in truth, speaks what He hears from Jesus, and foretells what is to come.
(John 16:13-15)

The Holy Spirit is a seal in the lives of believers, who confirms us as God's children and guarantees eternal life.
(Ephesians 1:1)

ROLES OF THE HOLY SPIRIT

The Holy Spirit is the Advocate, who teaches and reminds of what Jesus said and did, and bears witness or testifies of Jesus.

(John 14:26, John 15:26)

The Holy Spirit is a Helper, who helps in our weakness and prays for us.

(Romans 8:26-27)

The Holy Spirit convicts the world of sin.

(John 16:7-8)

The Holy Spirit sanctifies and enables good fruit in the lives of believers.

(Galatians 5:16-25)

The Holy Spirit manifests for the common good by giving spiritual gifts to believers.

(1 Corinthians 12:7-11)

The Holy Spirit empowers Christians for witnessing and defending the Christian faith.

(Mark 13:11; Luke 12:11-12; Matthew 10:19-20; Acts 1:8)

Chapter 11 - Jesus Christ Suffers

We come now to Jesus' suffering. He was prophesied to be the Suffering Servant. The prophecy foretold the suffering Jesus Christ, the Messiah, would endure. It is the part of Jesus' life we don't want to hear about or believe; it's brutal, evil, and cruel what Jesus endured. The verse below tells us, *"He was a man of sorrows, familiar with grief."* Wow!

When you can, read the full prophecy. Also, consider reading this chapter at your convenience, when you can follow and absorb it, as well as Isaiah 52:13 and Psalm 22:1-31.

As you read this chapter, think of all the good I shared about Jesus, the sermons He preached, the people He healed, the sins He forgave, and all the people He touched. One would think He would be on some kind of spiritual high doing all this. We are happy when we help others and they get better. But it says Jesus was "a man of sorrows, familiar with grief." All while He was preaching, touching, and changing lives, He was feeling sorrow. Was Jesus carrying our sorrow? Was He feeling the grief of humankind's sin? Was He depressed? Or sorrowful from the constant harassment He was enduring? Maybe a theologian reading this will send me an answer.

Isaiah 53 (ESV) reads about Jesus Christ:

... He had no form or majesty that we should look at him, and no beauty that we should desire him.
He was despised and rejected by men; a man of sorrows and acquainted with grief; and as one from whom men hide their faces
He was despised, and we esteemed him not.
Surely he has borne our griefs *and carried our sorrows;*
Yet we esteemed him stricken, smitten by God, and afflicted.
But he was wounded for our transgressions.
He was crushed for our iniquities.
Upon him was the chastisement that brought us peace...
He was oppressed, and he was afflicted, yet he opened not his mouth; like a lamb that is led to the slaughter,
and like a sheep that before its shearers is silent, so he opened not his mouth.

By oppression and judgment, he was taken away.
And as for his generation, who considered that he was cut off out of the land of the living, stricken for the transgression of my people?...
They made his grave with the wicked and with a rich man in his death, although he had done no violence,
And there was no deceit in his mouth.
Yet it was the will of the Lord to crush him; He has put him to grief...
Because he poured out his soul to death and was numbered with the transgressors...

Author and Pastor, Jay Y. Kim writes in an article on Faithway.com:

> There is a human tendency to place ourselves at the center of our own little universe. With piercingly beautiful words and Spirit-inspired clarity, the apostle Paul declares that there is only one center around which a faithful Christian can orbit and not have life spin out of control. Jesus, the divine One, is our center... More than 2,000 years ago, an itinerant rabbi with no home, no political influence, and no formal religious organization claimed to be 'the way, the truth and the life' (John 14:6)... The religious leaders of the day were so convinced that Jesus was claiming to be God, and the only way to eternal life with the Father, they had Him nailed to a Roman cross. They delighted as His blood poured to the ground and His life was snuffed out after only thirty-three years walking on this earth. When Jesus declared He was the divine center of all things, He made the boldest claim in the history of the world (Kim).

I pondered what Pastor Jay says here, "There is a human tendency to place ourselves at the center of our own little universe, [but] the apostle Paul declares that there is only one center around which a faithful Christian can orbit and not have life spin out of control." How true this is, how significant. This is how I was — the center of my life. As Christians who follow Jesus, we can never put ourselves on a plateau (as it seems today's Christians are doing), be selfish, and think only of ourselves. We falter, fail, and are not perfect. We do not always tell the truth or live honest lives. Our motives are not always pure. Jesus, however, suffered to death for being good and telling the truth about who He was. We will never top Him and should never put ourselves before Him or make people think we are equal to Jesus Christ. OMG!

This description of Jesus does not depict a man of nobility or regality, having a glorious, radiant life, free of challenges or struggles, does it? Rather, these verses of scripture suggest someone who is a misfit, an outsider, an unacceptable troublemaker. Jesus was not, yet it says, He was rejected, bullied, beaten, unfairly treated, forsaken, maligned, lied about, teased, and not believed; experiences that many of us may relate to in life.

No one in history has been as wrongfully accused, abused, or betrayed as Jesus Christ, who always did good. Isaiah 53 says, *Yet it was the will of the Lord to crush him; He has put him to grief.* Why would God the Father want Jesus to suffer so badly? We can't comprehend this. We struggle to understand our own painful suffering. We ask God, "Why?" don't we?

What difficult experiences are you facing, or have faced? Have you been tormented, bullied, or shamed? Have you done well but received wrong, or been mocked, shamed, and lied about? Have you experienced abandonment that left you feeling lonely? Have you experienced physical pain, loss, or rejection after showing love? Did anyone or any institution treat you unjustly or stereotype you? Has anyone cared about what happened to you? Have you suffered injustice because of a faulty legal system or prejudice? Were you ever betrayed or heartbroken? Did something crush your dreams, or did you lose hope? Are you serving a prison sentence for a crime you did not commit? If so, this part of Jesus' story should resonate and touch you—He was the Suffering Servant.

The Old Testament prophet Isaiah was to write about Jesus Christ, the Messiah, detailing what He would endure and all He would go through on earth. Perhaps you watched a movie that depicted this tumultuous time in Jesus' life. Maybe you follow the story every year during the Easter or Lenten season. You read His story to commemorate the sacrifice Jesus Christ paid for us. Sacrifice, you say? Yes. This climax to Jesus' life was just that—a sacrifice. Why? Because we are born to live. Jesus Christ was born to die—and He knew this.

Jesus Christ's suffering and death was a willing sacrifice He made for all people. He had us in mind during His suffering. Jesus served the world by enduring this suffering, because it was the only way to bring salvation to humanity. Unlike us, Jesus accepted this purpose because it was God's will.

If you are familiar with or have already read this part about Jesus' life, follow it here with me; I inject some comments you may not have thought about or heard before. If it's your first time hearing about this part of Jesus' journey, good. Jesus' severe suffering went like this.

The Rubber Meets the Road

The time is approaching. The time to be a man of your word is about to unfold. The climactic events that Jesus told His closest followers about are about to happen. They should hold on to their seats, guard their hearts, and keep their faith. They would face a decisive moment, when Jesus' teachings, preaching, and proclamations about God would all be put on the line. After caring for, loving, and touching so many people, this would be the worst season of Jesus' life. Many were unsympathetic and wanted this "new kid on the block" gone; to them, he was a threat and nothing but a troublemaker (Mark 3:6). Their hatred of Jesus had mounted to the point of their putting a plan in motion to get rid of Him.

Would Jesus now succumb to fear and bail out, back down, and take back His own will and revert His "Yes" to God to a "No." No, He wouldn't. Of His own free will, Jesus would give up His rights and face torment, lay down His life, and die a criminal's death.

Through these unfolding events, you will see how Jesus, through suffering, would now prove that He really is the Messiah, King. He would show that He was more than just a religious leader, rabbi, minister, or priest. Jesus would show total trust in and love for God and humanity. His actions would prove His love and show how serious He was when teaching about "laying down one's life for a friend," "denying oneself," and "taking up a cross." This is the crux of the Christian message, and Jesus models it for us.

Jesus Christ Predicts His Suffering and Death

Jesus predicted His time of suffering and told His disciples about it on several occasions; they did not understand what He meant or didn't want to accept it. Jesus wanted them to be prepared for what they were about to witness. They were His loyal friends and followers, and He cared about how they might feel once events unfolded. One of them, Peter, told Jesus that "this would never be" (Matthew 16:22). Peter was only thinking as any close friend would. Peter probably thought, "Jesus, as long as you have us, we will let nothing happen to you. We got you." Ironically, Jesus recognizes that Satan is using Peter, and He rebukes him. Jesus knew it was God's will for Him to suffer and had to keep this perspective. Well-intentioned friends *can* thwart God's plan for us, especially if it seems odd or "off the cuff." You must look past what friends or family may think when you are serving God. His will and plan trump the desires of friends or family. Imagine if Jesus were so into His disciples, leaned to their point of view, and said, "You know what, Peter, you are right; I'm the Messiah, king of Israel. Why should I have to suffer like this? This is not right."

You can read Jesus' predictions of his betrayal and death in Matthew 16:21-28, 17:22-23, 20:17-19; Mark 8:31-33, 9:30-32, 10:32-34; and Luke 9:22, 9:43-45, 18:31-34.

Jesus Struggles and Questions God

As we do, Jesus struggled with this sad ordeal and asked God, "Why?" There is a point at which Jesus becomes sorrowful and apprehensive about the climax to His life. He's thinking about and bothered by the suffering He's about to endure and goes to talk with God about it. He takes some of His disciples with Him to pray with Him. Jesus Christ asks God, the Father, if there was any other way this could be done; could He avoid this? He asks God if this "cup" (of suffering) could be taken from Him. Suffering and pain are unpleasant; we dislike them. If we could, we would exchange places with someone who's doing okay, right? Jesus can relate. He, too, wished not to go through any agony or death. God obviously told Him, "No." This was the way for H to go, the thing He had to do. Jesus submits to God's will, arises from prayer, and says, in essence, "Okay, Father, I will. Let's do it!" **(Read this in Mark 14:32-42.)**

Jesus Faces Betrayal

Jesus first faces betrayal in the Garden of Gethsemane. At His most difficult moment, as He was agonizing over the suffering ahead, He prayed and asked His disciples to pray as well. He was surely wrestling with and having a difficult time grasping this entire ordeal, feeling the pain of it before it even happened. He needed His friends to pray with Him, give Him strength, and offer encouragement. They didn't. They all fell asleep while He was sweating in agony. I'm sure that disappointed Jesus. **(Read about this in Matthew 26:36-46.)**

The disciples betray Jesus even more. Jesus knew that this betrayal was going to happen. Have you ever sensed a hater in your inner circle, but they don't know that you know? So did Jesus. It's interesting that while walking, teaching, dining, and communicating with them, Jesus knew all along who His haters were and who would betray Him. Jesus tells them they would betray Him; the disciples are distressed about this. They insisted they would never do such a thing. Peter and Judas Iscariot are the two that Jesus singled out as betrayers.

(Jesus' prediction about His betrayers is in Matthew 26:17-25; Mark 14:17-21; Luke 22:7-23; and John 13:18-30.)

-*Simon Peter* is the disciple whom Jesus told that he would deny Him. Peter tells Jesus he would die for Him if it came to that. Peter was a bold, boisterous, outspoken, loyal, and confident disciple. He was going to be Jesus' "ride or die" partner. However, as the crowds began turning on Jesus, so did Peter; He acted as if he didn't know Him and began to curse and swear about it. I told you earlier, never say, "I'll never."

(This prediction of Peter's denial is in Matthew 26:31-35; Mark 14:27-31, Luke 22:31-34; John 13:31-38; and in Matthew 26:69-75; Mark 14:66-72; Luke 22:56-62; John 18:15-18, 25-27 shows his actual denial.)

Later, Peter was devastated and crushed, and he cried bitterly because he had denied His friend, the Lord.

-*Judas Iscariot.* Judas not only betrays Jesus but also hands Him over to be arrested. Interestingly, Jesus doesn't stop him, chase after him, fight him, give him a sermon to change his mind, or pray for him. Instead, He says to him, *Do what you have to do.* Jesus seems resolved in letting the pre-planned events unfold.

(Read it in Matthew 26:47-56; Mark 14:43-50; Luke 22:47-48.)

-All the disciples flee and leave Jesus alone. **(Matthew 26:56; Mark 14:50; Luke 23:49.)**

-The people Jesus helped/healed/forgave/delivered. From being amazed by Jesus' words and acts, the crowds He helped became appalled by Him. After thanking and glorifying Him, they changed to yelling, *Crucify Him.* I guess, they became disappointed when they realized Jesus was not there to set them free from Roman bondage, so they joined the crowd who thought He was a criminal and demanded He die. Only recently, they welcomed Him in Jerusalem and hailed Him as the Messiah, King of the Jews. Now, seeing H presume they thought, "No king is going to take this. Kings are powerful." It's difficult when someone you've given everything to betrays or changes their mind about you, especially after you've always stood by them and loved them. They don't want you anymore.

Nothing hurts or is more grievous than when a friend hurts you or a foe, disguised as a friend, blindsides you in life. It cuts straight through your heart, and you wonder, "What did I do?" King David expresses this sentiment about a friend who betrayed him in Psalm 55. His experience is a reflection of Jesus' betrayal by one of His own disciples. From an enemy, one expects hostility, but not from a friend. All these betrayed Jesus, forsook him, and looked the other way. Jesus had no defense and was all alone. He kept on going though.

Jesus Arrested and Imprisoned

It was the disciple Judas who handed Jesus over to be arrested by the religious authorities for a sum of money (30 pieces of silver). Just after having dinner with Him, he sold Him out. He tells the religious leaders they would know who Jesus is when he kisses Him. A kiss? Now, that's cold! How cunning, right? A crowd armed with clubs and swords sent by the chief priests, experts in the law, and elders, searches for Jesus, with Judas leading the pack.

(Read this account in Matthew 26:14-16; Mark 14:10-11; Luke 22:1-6; John 13:2 and Matthew 26:47-50; Mark 14:42-46; Luke 22:47-48.)

Notice how Jesus does not begin fighting or attempt to run and hide from the authorities. He willingly reveals Himself by saying, *I am Jesus whom you are looking for... 'Have you come out with swords and clubs to arrest me like you would an outlaw? Day after day, I was teaching in the temple courts, yet you did not arrest me. But this has happened so that the scriptures of the prophets would be fulfilled. Then all the disciples left him and fled* **(Matthew 26:55-56).**

Notice, too, how all the disciples flee when the heat is on. It's like the police showing up in our neighborhood or at a friend's home. We tell the cops or our friends, "Look, we have nothing to do with this; we don't want any part." They walk away so as not to get into any trouble and never come close to help.

Jesus on Trial in (6) Illegal Court Proceedings

Are you reading this from a prison cell for a crime you didn't commit? Jesus was innocent, too. Your trial or legal proceedings may have been unfair. Law enforcement mishandled, handcuffed, and beat Jesus, and the legal system treated Him as guilty before proving Him innocent.

Jesus' trial was illegal for several reasons. I learned that: (1) Jesus was arrested without being charged or accused of any offense against Jewish law; (2) Jewish law prohibited nighttime and one-day trials; (3) false witnesses told lies about what Jesus said and did; (4) the location of the trial was incorrect; (5) Judas received money from the religious establishment for turning Jesus in; (6) the Sanhedrin arrested Jesus during Passover; (7) and the religious establishment changed the charges against Jesus in order to have Him killed because under Jewish law they could not have Him crucified. Only Rome could order his killing.

It's essential to recognize the diverse ways in which the biblical authors portray Jesus' suffering during this period. One author records in more detail what another doesn't. Their facts agree, however.

The emphasis here is to highlight the unjust sufferings Jesus endured from the time of His initial arrest. Jesus' trial was illegal, and His treatment was brutal and unfair. They shift Jesus here and there, and several Roman officials and the Jewish religious establishment question Him. Below, the numbers identify each official and entity before whom Jesus stood. Pay attention to the bullet points.

(Read these accounts in Matthew 26:44-50; Mark 14:43-50; Luke 22:47-53; John 18:3-12.)

1. ***Before Annas*** - **(John 18:12-13, 19-24)**

He was the father-in-law of Caiaphas, who was the high priest that year. Annas was the patriarch of a family line of high priests who succeeded him. Still referred to as "the high priest" (Acts 4:6), he clung to the reins of control and was the wealthy kingpin of the moneychangers and merchants in the temple. Jesus' cleansing of the temple was a direct challenge to Annas' authority. In this trial, Jesus experienced:

- Soldiers, along with the commander and Jewish officials, arrest Jesus.
- Tied him up.
- The high priest questions Jesus about His disciples and about His teachings.
- Jesus declares He always spoke openly in public and taught in the temple and synagogue where Jews assemble; He tells them to ask them because they know.
- An officer of the high priest strikes Jesus in the face because of the reply He made. His reason for striking Him was, *Is that the way you answer the high priest? Jesus replies, If I have done something wrong, confirm what is wrong. But if I spoke correctly, why strike me?*
- Annas sends Jesus to Caiaphas, the high priest.

2. ***Before Caiphas and the teachers of the law and the elders*** **- (Matthew 26:57-75; Mark 14:53–65; Luke 22:54-71; John 18:14)**
   - The chief priests and the entire Sanhedrin sought evidence against Jesus but found none.

- Gave false testimony against Him and distorted Jesus' words.
- Jesus is silent and gives no answer. *Then the high priest stood up before the man and asked Jesus, Have you no answer? What is this that they are testifying against you?*
- The high priests question Jesus, *Are you the Messiah, the Son of the Blessed One?* Now Jesus replies, *I am, and you will see the Son of Man sitting at the right hand of the Mighty One and coming on the clouds of heaven.* He maintains His identity and does not back down.
- The high priests became offended after this statement and called for an immediate verdict. *Then the high priest tore his clothes and said, Why do we still need witnesses? You have heard the blasphemy!' What is your verdict?*
- The authorities condemn Jesus to death.
- They spat on Jesus.
- They blindfold Him.
- They strike Him with their fists and mock Him, saying, *Prophesy!*
- The guards brutalized Him.
- They insult Jesus.

3. ***Before the Sanhedrin*** -

   (Matthew 26:57-68; Mark 14:53-63; Luke 22:54-71)

   - The council of the elders of the people—both the chief priests and the experts in the law — questions Jesus. *If you are the Christ, tell us. Jesus says to them, If I tell you, you will not believe, and if I ask you, you will not answer. But from now on the Son of Man will be seated at the right hand of the power of God.*
   - Again, Jesus maintains His identity.
   - They ask, *Are you the Son of God, then?* He answers them; *You say that I am.* They judged Jesus for blasphemy because He said this, which warranted stoning.
   - They concluded and immediately declared Jesus guilty with no need for further testimony.

4. ***Before Herod*** - the one who beheaded Jesus' cousin, John the Baptist **(Luke 23:6-12)**
    - Pilate learns Jesus is from Herod's jurisdiction and sends Him there.
    - Herod was glad because he had heard about Jesus and longed to see Him, hoping He would perform a miraculous sign.
    - Herod questions Jesus at considerable length, but Jesus gives him no answer.
    - The chief priests and the experts in the law were standing there accusing Jesus.
    - Herod and his soldiers mocked and treated Jesus with contempt.
    - They dress Jesus in elegant clothes, and Herod sends him back to Pilate.
    - Herod does not see Jesus as a threat to Rome.

Pilate and Herod had been enemies before this, but they had now become friends.

5&6. ***Before Pilate in Roman trials*** **- (Read these instances in Matthew 27:1-2, 11-14, 15-31; Mark 15:1-20; Luke 23:1-5, 13-25; John 18:28-40, 19:1-16)**

Pilate, the Roman governor, followed the Roman trial procedure: he presented the accusation, questioned the accused, heard the defense, and then made his judgment. Jesus Christ stood before him twice, as you will read in Scripture, because Herod sent him back to Pilate. I have compiled the events from both trials.

The religious establishment breaks its judicial laws. In their rush to judgment, these guardians of morality had broken almost every judicial code. According to the Talmud, trials were to be held during the daytime, in public, and not during a festival. The religious leaders, however, had tried Jesus at night and in secret during Passover week. They had no credible witnesses. Jesus had no defense attorney. The high priest himself led the questioning. The sentence was given without deliberation, and all violations of their own laws. They had their death sentence, but now needed the means to carry it out. Only the Romans could execute criminals, so the Jewish leaders took Jesus to Pontius Pilate to try the case.

- They take Jesus into the governor's residence, where a whole cohort of soldiers circles Him. (That's about 500 to 600 soldiers.)
- Because of ceremonial customs, the religious establishment does not enter. Pilate meets them outside to find out the accusation against Jesus.
- They declare Jesus a criminal and tell Pilate, *We would not have handed him over to you if He weren't a criminal.* (This is a lie.)
- Pilate tells them to try Jesus according to their customs, but they cannot put Him to death legally.
- They lie again in Luke 23:1-2. *Then the whole group of them rose and brought Jesus before Pilate. They began to accuse him, saying; We found this man subverting our nation, forbidding us to pay the tribute tax to Caesar and claiming that he himself is Christ, a king.* (Jesus had this discussion about paying taxes. (See Matthew 22:15-22.)
- Pilate questions Jesus about being a king. Once again, Jesus maintains His identity and, in so many words, says yes.
- Pilate finds no basis for their accusations. Three times, he says Jesus is not worthy of death. He asks them, *What evil has he done?*
- The religious establishment persists in saying that Jesus started riots among the people with His teachings.
- Pilate tells Jesus that it was His own people who handed Him over and asks Him, *What have you done?* Jesus gives Pilate a sermon, somewhat, on where His kingdom is.
- Pilate asserts that Jesus acknowledged being a king. Pilate asks Jesus, *What is truth?* Again, Jesus gives him a sort of sermon on truth.
- Pilate follows the Jewish custom to release one prisoner at the Passover. He asks if they want him to release Jesus, King of the Jews, or Barabbas, a criminal. The crowds demanded Barabbas' release but

Jesus' crucifixion. Have we/Do we demand Barabbas (the wrong) instead of Jesus?

- Pilate had Jesus severely flogged by the Roman officials. This was the standard punishment for those sentenced to crucifixion.

  Flogging involves two men using a leather whip with bone and lead on the ends. The whip forcefully comes down on the body, first tearing the skin, and then, with each hit, cutting deeper into the tissues, muscles, and veins. The body oozes a lot of blood and becomes unrecognizable. Romans had no limit on the number of strikes they could do.

- Soldiers strip Jesus' clothes, put a scarlet robe around Him, and put a braided crown of thorns on His head.
- They mock Jesus by putting a staff in His right hand and kneeling before Him, facetiously saying, *Hail, King of the Jews!*
- They spit on Him and strike Him repeatedly on His head with a staff.
- They strike Jesus repeatedly in the face.
- The crowd shouts, *Crucify him.* Jewish leaders say, *We have a law, and according to our law, he ought to die because he claimed to be the Son of God!*
- Pilate becomes fearful and questions Jesus, *Where do you come from?* Jesus does not answer.
- Pilate asserts his authority over Jesus. Jesus replies, *You would have no authority over me at all unless it were given to you from above.*
- Pilate tries his best to set Jesus free, but the Jewish leaders put pressure on him and use his being a friend to Caesar as a reason he should not release Jesus. They were adamant. By any means necessary, they would have Jesus killed.
- Pilate sits on the judgment seat and presents Jesus to them. He says, *Look, here is your king!*
- They yell, *Away with him! Away with him! Crucify him!*

- Pilate asks them, *Shall I crucify your king?* The chief priests respond, *We have no king but Caesar.* They wanted to remain in good standing with the Roman government.
- Finally, Pilate gives in, releases Barabbas, and hands Jesus over to be crucified.
- Pilate washes his hands of this act based on a dream his wife had and because a riot was now starting. **(See Matthew 27:24-26.)** He says, *I am innocent of this man's blood. You take care of yourselves!*
- The crowd replies, *Let his blood be on us and on our children!*
- Soldiers put Jesus' own clothes back on Him and led Him away to be crucified. Imagine how Jesus' body felt having cloth on His skin, after being flogged and His skin ripped open; it probably stung.

Jesus Nailed to a Cross

(Read Matthew 27:32-56; Mark 15:21-41; Luke 23:26-49; John 19:28-37.)

Crucifixion was the worst form of death at that time. It had all the most needed areas of torture and was an unforgettable death. Devised in honor of a pagan god, all pagan societies embraced it, and it continued until Constantine. The crucifixion victim sat in the middle of the square among military soldiers. The criminal carried his cross with the crime written on a titulus, a piece of wood, around his neck. All the people would know what the crime was (Google A.I.).

Pilate had a notice written and fastened to Jesus' cross, which read: *Jesus the Nazarene, the King of the Jews.* Because they crucified Jesus in the city, many Jewish residents read the notice, which was in Aramaic, Latin, and Greek. The Pharisees disagree about this. They wanted it to read, *He said he was King of the Jews* (John 19:21). Pilate leaves the notice as he had written it.

Outside the city walls, a vertical beam and a crossbeam are uniquely prepared for the victim. The cross's horizontal crosspiece, called the *patibulum*, would have been placed on Jesus' shoulders to carry.

Surrounded by four Roman soldiers and led by a centurion, Jesus was paraded through busy city streets to the site of the crucifixion just outside of town. **(Matthew**

27:32–34 describes the way to Golgotha.)

- Crucifixion is the most painful, humiliating, shameful, and torturous form of death.
- It is the slowest form of death and the most public.
- "Crucifixion was so horrible that it was reserved for only the worst offenders," (GotQuestions.org).
- Carrying his own cross, Jesus walks to a place called "The Place of the Skull" (in Aramaic, *Golgotha*).
- A man is selected to help Jesus carry His cross because surely, after all the severe hits, beatings, and flogging, Jesus was weak, in pain, limp, delirious, and half dead.
- They offer Jesus sour wine to drink, but He doesn't drink it.
- They divided Jesus' garments and cast lots.
- The soldiers placed Jesus between two thieves, also being crucified. One of them knows Jesus is innocent and asks to be with Him when He comes into His kingdom; Jesus grants his request because he believed in who He was.
- Passersby insult Jesus: *If you are the Son of God, then save yourself.*
- The chief priest and elders mock Jesus, saying, *He saved others but can't save Himself. If you are a king, come down from the cross and we'll believe. He trusted God; let Him deliver him now.*
- Jesus prays to the Father to forgive them; they didn't know what they were doing.
- Jesus makes provision for His mother to be cared for by the disciple, John.
- Jesus, realizing that by this time everything was completed, says (in order to fulfill the scripture), *I am thirsty!* A jar of sour wine was there, so they put a sponge soaked in sour wine on a branch of hyssop and lifted it to His mouth.
- From the sixth to the ninth hour, there is darkness over the land.
- At the 9th hour, Jesus cries out in Aramaic, *Eli, Eli, lama Sabachthani*, which means, *My God, my God, why have you forsaken me?* People

think He is calling on the Old Testament prophet, Elijah, but some say, *Leave him alone; let's see if Elijah comes to save him.*

- Familiar women are there watching and mourning: Mary Magdalene, Mary the mother of James, Salome, and many other women. Jesus tells them not to weep for Him.
- They pounce with great thrust nails through Jesus' hands and feet. I wonder at this point if Jesus could even feel the pounding of the nails because His body had gone numb?

It was a gruesome, tumultuous, crushing time in Jerusalem for Jesus' followers and His mother. Remember, she raised Him well in the Jewish law.

Can you feel Jesus' pain? Do you feel sorrow for Him after hearing all the good we've read about Him? Are you crying? Here is the man who obeyed all the Jewish laws, always did things that pleased God, and who always went around teaching and doing good for people. Now, He's on a cross, sentenced as a criminal, beaten beyond recognition, and about to die. OMG!

But Jesus hasn't died yet. He has a couple of more things to take care of.

Pastor Ray Stedman writes about why the cross was necessary. In his daily devotion, The Necessity of the Cross, he states:

> Christianity without the cross is not Christianity at all, but a shabby, slimy substitute. The word of the cross is what makes it Christian. What does it mean?... First, it means the end of the natural, the end of what we call self-sufficiency... The word of the cross means the end of all our reliance upon ourselves, and we dislike that... The second element involves pain and hurt. It always does because we do not like being cut off ... The third element of the way of the cross is that it leads to a resurrection... They seemed arrested by the cross and could never get beyond it ... But the way of the cross always leads to a resurrection, to a new beginning, on different terms. (Stedman, The Necessity of the Cross)

Jesus Dies

(Read this in Matthew 27:45-56; Mark 15:33-41; Luke 23:44-49; John 19:28-30.)

Before Jesus dies, He says and does something:

- Jesus cries out in Aramaic, *Eli, Eli, lama Sabachthani,* which means, *My God, My God, why have you forsaken me?* Jesus asks God a "why" question?
- Jesus says, *I am thirsty.* They lift a sponge with vinegar to His mouth.
- Jesus proclaims, *It is finished.*

The Meaning of "It is Finished"

What did Jesus mean when He said, "It is finished?" Did He mean His life was over? Was He referring to His body, which was about to expire, or something else? In the Jesus Bible, NIV Edition, it states:

> It is finished"—a simple sentence, made of only three simple words, but the significance of this sentence has eternal consequences for billions of people. When Jesus declares, "It is finished," he indicates that his work of salvation is finished; that he has paid the full price for our sins. The cross is about so much more than a man enduring pain and suffering; it is about so much more than a man being abandoned by his friends and family. The cross is about Jesus, the eternal Son of God, being forsaken by his Father. Jesus, who had forever been one with the Father, was willing to come to earth and identify with sinners like us. He was even willing to become our sin (2 Co. 5:21), so that on the cross he could die in our place. On the cross, the hellish punishment that we deserved was placed on him; he willingly endured God's wrath in order to set us free." (The NIV Jesus Bible)

"It is Finished" resulted in:

- Completion of salvation: Jesus' words mean the work of salvation is completely finished. It signifies that the price for humanity's sins has been fully paid.
- Fulfillment of God's plan: The phrase marks the culmination of God's plan as laid out in scripture.
- "It is finished" is a phrase that means "paid in full," indicating that there is nothing more to be done to earn salvation.
- A cry of victory: It is considered a cry of triumph rather than defeat, announcing victory over sin, death, and the powers of darkness.
- An act of obedience: The statement also represents the full obedience of Jesus to the will of the Father, even through immense suffering (Google A.I.).

- Jesus also says, *Father, into your hands I commit my spirit.* Much of the weight and significance of this sentence lies in the fact that Jesus is communicating with the Father, indicating that He is returning to His side. After thirty-three years of earthly ministry, and the Father briefly turning away during the Crucifixion in Mark 15:34, when the Lord cries out, "Eli, Eli, lama Sabachthani?" which means, "My God, my God, why have you forsaken me?" It is also significant because of its connection to Psalm 31:3-5; it's a direct quotation from that passage.

- Jesus releases or gives up His spirit and dies. The term "gave up" emphasizes the voluntary nature of Jesus' self-sacrifice (see note on John 10:17) and echoes Isaiah 53:12—his spirit. Jesus' human spirit, which He voluntarily released from His body so that it might return to God the Father's presence (see Luke 23:43, 46)." (The ESV Global Study Bible).

- What Jesus did: *"He bowed his head and gave up the ghost*. He was voluntary in dying; for he was not only the sacrifice, but the priest and the offerer ... Christ showed his will in his sufferings, *by which will we are sanctified*. (1.) *He gave up the ghost*. His life was not forcibly taken from

> him, but rather freely given up. He had said, *Father, into thy hands I commit my spirit*, thereby expressing the intention of this act. I give up myself as a ransom *for many*; and, accordingly, he did give up his spirit, paid down the price of pardon and life at his Father's hands. Father, *glorify thy name*. (2.) *He bowed his head* ... The bowing of his head shows his submission to his Father's will, and his obedience unto death... He accommodated himself to his dying work. (Matthew Henry's Commentary on the Bible)

- A soldier pierces Jesus' side; blood and water protrude, which proves His humanity (John 19:34).
- Witnesses "beat their breasts (a gesture of grief, sorrow, remorse, and repentance) and leave.

Wow!

Interesting Facts After Jesus Dies

Upon Jesus' final breath, scripture records some interesting things that happened. **(See Matthew 27:50-54.)**

- The Jewish temple curtain is torn in two, which signifies that the religious rules and acts are no longer in effect; they are no longer needed. This is significant because the veil of the temple separated the holy place, where God resides, from the people.
- The earth shook and rocks split (earthquake); defies nature.
- Dead bodies rise and come to life (miracles).
- Centurions and guards are fearful after seeing this. They now believe and say, *Truly this one was God's Son!* (They now show faith in Him.)

Jesus is Buried

(Read this in Matthew 27:57-66; Mark 15:42-47; Luke 23:50-56; John 19:38-42.) Just like the gravesite services we attend for our loved ones, Jesus' body too was placed in a grave. He understands the sadness we feel.

- A rich man from Arimathea, named Joseph, who was also a disciple of Jesus, requests Jesus' body from Pilate. Pilate orders it to be given to him. Joseph wraps Jesus' body in a clean linen cloth with spices, and places it in his own new tomb that he had cut in the rock, where no one had ever been buried. He rolled a huge stone across the entrance of the tomb.
- Nicodemus, whom Jesus once talked with, came and brought a mixture of myrrh and aloes.
- Mary Magdalene and Mary, the mother of Jesus, see where He was laid and return home to prepare spices and ointments, but rest because it was the Sabbath.
- The chief priests and Pharisees are tenacious. They wanted Pilate to have guards watch Jesus' tomb. They reminded him that Jesus, while alive, had said He would come back to life after three days. They say, *Otherwise, his disciples may come and steal his body and say to the people, He has been raised from the dead, and the last deception will be worse than the first.*

  You would think by now they would be satisfied that Jesus is dead, but they are tenacious. The request for a guard at His tomb reveals their deeper spiritual problem. They wanted everyone to believe as they did—that Jesus was a fake and His words untrue; He was not the promised Messiah, King. They knew that if what Jesus spoke happened, He would prove all He was proclaiming to be. OMG!

- Pilate accommodates them and says, *Take a guard of soldiers. Go and make it as secure as you can. So, they went with the soldiers of the guard and made the tomb secure by sealing the stone.*

Think About It—Why Death?

This was such a sacrificial act that no one else could have or would have faced—or ever will. But Jesus Christ willingly faced the torment and pain, sacrificed and shed His blood, thus earning the rank as ruler of God's kingdom forever and ever. I probably wouldn't have made it through that successfully. I get upset sometimes just if someone looks at me the wrong way. I would have been kicking, screaming, complaining, and cussing. Isn't that how we sometimes handle painful ordeals today? We watch the news and see people rallying and protesting for their cause.

We also read how, despite their heroics, bravery, and nobility, the journeys of all heroes, prominent leaders, noblemen, and people climax in death. No matter their exceptional gifts or contributions to others. No matter the accolades given to them by society or the talents/skills that contributed to its change and growth. Their contributions and existence end. Jesus' life did too, you may say. He also died and was buried. So, is that it? Is that where things end? Nope.

Regarding Jesus Christ's death, and in response to the scripture in Hebrews 9:15-22, Pastor Ray Stedman writes in one of his daily devotionals, "The Need for Death":

> We shall never come to the answer until we squarely face the implications of the substitutionary character of the death of Jesus Christ. His death was not for his own sake, it was for ours. He was our representative. This is what God is so desperately trying to convey to us... The cross is God's way of saying there is nothing in us worth saving at all, if we remain set apart from Christ. As we were, men and women quite apart from Christ, God says, There is nothing you can do for me, not one thing. But when Christ became what we were, when he was made sin for us, God passed sentence upon him and put him to death. This is God's way of saying to us, There is not a thing you can do by your own effort that is worth a thing. All that we can ever be without Christ is totally set aside. Death eliminates us, wipes us out... Father... teach me to grasp this and to accept thy sentence of death upon everything in me that is not of Christ (Stedman).

All along, it was the aim of Jesus' haters and accusers, as well as the devil, when he tempted Jesus in the wilderness—to stop Jesus from suffering and dying. But Jesus did not take the bait and give in. He never stopped being or declaring who He was, even though He knew what the ultimate cost would be. Had He sided with and given in to His haters' claims, the mission would have been in vain, flawed, and incomplete. The sacrifice needed for our salvation would have been prevented. Jesus never aborted God's plan for saving us. Yes, it was sacrificial because He had you and me in mind all the while He was going through this.

The prophecy in Isaiah 53, the verse we looked at previously, explains in verses 5-7 what this was all for. It says, *He was despised, and we considered him insignificant. But he lifted up our illnesses; he carried our pain; even though we thought he was being punished, attacked by God, and afflicted for something he had done. He was wounded because of our rebellious deeds, crushed because of our sins; he endured punishment that made us well; because of his wounds, we have been healed.*

The Bible also declares in Romans 5:7-10 (NIV), *Very rarely will anyone die for a righteous person, though for a good person, someone might possibly dare to die. But God demonstrates his own love for us in this: while we were still sinners, Christ died for us. Since we have now been justified by his blood, how much more shall we be saved from God's wrath through him? For if, while we were God's enemies, we were reconciled to him through the death of his Son, how much more, having been reconciled, shall we be saved through his life!*

OMG! Let that sink in! I don't know about you, but I've never known a love like this before!

I concur; it is rare indeed that anyone endures such hardship, cruelty, and belittlement and suffers and dies for another; possibly for someone we like or love, we may. So, Jesus needs to be upfront—at the center of everything—if we say we are followers of His.

So, here it is, Christians--the model—which seems to emphasize 1 Corinthians 15:58 about remaining steadfast, being undeterred, and always abounding in God's service (regardless of what). Remaining who we are. Gaining the correct, broader perspective in all we go through. It's important to note that the aim of bullying, harassment, mockery, or abuse is to make the target think less of themselves, throw them off course, and cause them to believe something is mistaken with their identity to get them to change or lean to their side. Their truth about themselves is flawed, so they should change and stop being who they are. Middle and high school students remember this.

We needed to hear about Jesus Christ, the man, in action and all He suffered. We needed to know what He modeled for us to follow, to become like. The prophecies about Jesus hailed Him as King, Savior of the World, and Prince of Peace. Still, it was through struggle, pain, and death He would receive these ranks. It *is the way we are to think and be.*

This is the way for a Christian, the way to live the Christian life. Jesus did it first to show us how. Life in Christ involves losing to win, giving up to gain, relinquishing to keep, and denying to finding truth. This is totally counterintuitive to how the world thinks and acts. This is God's way, God's path to life and blessing in Him, and it's how the kingdom of God operates. It's why I rarely use the word 'success' about the Christian journey because it's not a contest—about being the most successful, outperforming competitors, being on top, winning prizes. No.

The Bible Project team also has another excellent blog you may enjoy reading. It's entitled "Why Did Jesus Have to Die? (A Question Worth Unpacking). How the Biblical Story Helps Explain the Meaning of the Cross." Again, visit their main website at https://bibleproject.com/ and search for the blog title.

Abuses Jesus Experienced

There is no way to put in sequence or cover all the abuse Jesus experienced, but most are recorded, although not in detail. Several groups of people caused Jesus' pain, such as the Roman government, soldiers, Jewish leaders, the people he aided, and, sadly, His own disciples. All, ironically, joined forces—intentionally or unknowingly — against Jesus to cause Him hurt, pain, torture, abandonment, and ultimately death. Because He was a man in the flesh, Jesus can relate to the pain and trouble we suffer. That makes Him an excellent person to talk to about ours.

Review the chart with definitions. All definitions retrieved from:
(NIH) *National Library of Medicine, National Center for Biotechnology Information*
(Neel Burton) The Psychology of Humiliation. What is humiliation, and can it ever be justified? (Neel Burton)
(BibleHub)

Abuses Jesus Suffered

EMOTIONAL/ PSYCHOLOGICAL ABUSE	Defining psychological abuse, a term often used interchangeably with emotional abuse, is difficult. The consequences of psychological abuse, regardless of how it is defined, differ depending on the context and the age of the victim. Like other types of abuse, it can be defined as intentional behavior to communicate to the victim that they have no value (i.e., they are worthless or unwanted) or something is wrong with them. Thus, emotional abuse includes acts that disturb the emotional health of the individual. Such acts include restricting a person's movements (e.g., where they can go and who they can interact with), denigration, ridicule, threats and intimidation, discrimination, rejection, and other nonphysical forms of hostile treatment.
INSTITUTIONAL ABUSE	Institutional abuse occurs when there is the mistreatment of a person from a system of power, such as a corporation, hospital, nursing facility, school, or religious organization.
PHYSICAL ABUSE	Occurs as part of a constellation of behaviors including authoritarian control, anxiety-provoking behavior, and physical hurt or discomfort that is perpetrated by any person close to the victim.... The most prevalent forms of physical abuse involve both physical punishment and domestic violence, which also affect children in the family, even if they are not the direct target... Cultural factors appear to strongly influence the nature of physical abuse in most countries, depending on whether hitting, punching, kicking, or beating is socially and legally acceptable.
VERBAL ABUSE	• Refers to regular and consistent belittling, name-calling, labeling, or ridicule of a person; but it may also include spoken threats.

Abuses Jesus Suffered

DISCRIMINATION ABUSE

Involves verbal abuse, derogatory remarks, or inappropriate use of language. Denying access to communication aids, not allowing access to an interpreter, signer, or lip-reader. Harassment or deliberate exclusion. Denying basic rights to healthcare, education, employment, and criminal.

INTELLECTUAL OR SPIRITUAL ABUSE

Intellectual or spiritual abuse refers to such behaviors as punishing someone for having different intellectual interests or religious beliefs from others in the family, preventing them from attending worship services, ridiculing their opinions, and the like. Jesus was rejected, discredited, challenged, dismissed, and threatened by the entire religious establishment because He preached new perspectives and views from that of Judaism, although at the age of 12 they were amazed at the wisdom and knowledge He had of the Torah.

HUMILIATION

Embarrassment, shame, guilt, and humiliation all imply the existence of value systems...
The Latin root of 'humiliation' is *humus*, which means 'earth' or 'dirt'. Humiliation involves abasement of honour and dignity and, with that, loss of status and standing.... Still today, humiliation is a common form of punishment, abuse, and oppression. .. It is in the nature of humiliation that it undermines the ability of victims to defend themselves against their aggressors.

MOCKERY

Mockery, in the biblical context, refers to the act of ridiculing, deriding, or making fun of someone or something, often with the intent to belittle or scorn. It is a behavior that is frequently condemned in Scripture, as it reflects a heart that is not aligned with the virtues of humility, love, and respect that are central to Christian teaching... [it] is often rooted in pride and a lack of empathy, and it can be a tool used by the enemy to sow discord and division.... While mockery is a behavior that is prevalent in human interactions, Scripture consistently portrays it as contrary to the character of God and the teachings of Christ. Believers are encouraged to guard their hearts and tongues, choosing instead to speak words that reflect the love and grace of the Gospel.

Chapter 12 - Back to the Forefront: What Will it Take?

Therefore, since we are surrounded by such a great cloud of witnesses, let us throw off everything that hinders and the sin that so easily entangles. And let us run with perseverance the race marked out for us, fixing our eyes on Jesus, the pioneer and perfecter of faith. For the joy set before him he endured the cross, scorning its shame, and sat down at the right hand of the throne of God.

(Hebrews 12:1-2 NIV)

So, my friend, that's the story of Jesus, the Christ. They are facts about Him as recorded in the Scriptures of the Holy Bible— "the document God chose to communicate to humankind." Jesus' story is unique, unlike any other in history. No other person has lived or affected lives as He has.

Jesus' story sounds like fiction to some. But it's not conceived or created in someone's mind. You won't realize this until you believe in Him. After you believe and accept in faith that His story is true, He will reveal H truth and prove His works in your life, as He did for me.

Some people read Jesus' story and think it's quite impressive. Society concludes and hails Jesus as an exceptional man; I hear the accolades afforded Him. Some read Jesus' story out of intellectual curiosity, for historical research, or just to gain knowledge to pass a school exam. Others study Jesus' story to produce documentaries, films, or books about Him. Even so, many only seek to refute it, challenge its inconsistencies, all to prove it a lie or wrong.

I shared Jesus' story with you, coupled with my own, to attest to truthfulness, but also to recall what He was all about. His story is true. In the same way that He called His first twelve disciples, trained and changed them; He did the same in my life. The same way He interacted and went up close to the people He encountered is the same closeness He has shown me. The same way He fed the hungry, cast out demonic spirits, lifted the crowds out of oppression and depression, is the same thing He did for my family and me. In the same way He told the people to go in peace because their sins are forgiven, He tells me the same thing every time I still mess up. No, my friend, this is not a fictional story about Jesus Christ. He is alive and still touching and impacting lives—now through the Holy Spirit, who is keeping His mission going. Jesus Christ is real!

I intentionally concluded Jesus Christ's story with His suffering and death, rather than His resurrection, because it is in this aspect of sharing in His life that we often want to skip, not realizing its significance. It is the part with today's "Christian" that Is not highlighted. Difficulty, suffering, pain, "going against the grain" is why disciples left Him then and leave Him now. This is a part of the fellowship with Jesus we have been called to—suffering and self-denial, becoming like Him in His death. It's where today many professed Christians have left Jesus and turned away; they don't even realize it. It's the part of Jesus' story that many are not preaching today. They are proclaiming another false gospel, leading people astray and filling them with false, worldly hopes. This significant part of Jesus' story is beautified or misconstrued and told as some kind of work of fiction that Christians should not take at face value. Why?

You see, after His suffering and death, God exalted Jesus Christ as Lord. This shift brought Jesus to the center of the Christian faith. Acknowledging Him as Lord means recognizing His authority over every aspect of life. This understanding provides the solution for returning Jesus to the forefront in our personal faith and in the wider Church. Philippians 2:8-11 (NIV) says, *And being found in appearance as a man, he humbled himself by becoming obedient to death even death on a cross! Therefore, God exalted him to the highest place and gave him the name that is above every name, that at the name of Jesus every knee should bow, in heaven and on earth and under the earth, and every tongue acknowledge that Jesus Christ is Lord, to the glory of God the Father.*

This high exaltation as "Lord" connotes rulership, dominion, and government. Every knee must bow to Him, and every tongue must confess that Jesus is Lord. We understand then that He is in charge and runs the affairs of God. We acknowledge, respect, honor, and obey Him as such. Confession of Jesus as Lord from your mouth, as well as believing in your heart, is required for salvation (Romans 10:9).

As "the Christ," we believe He is the anointed Messiah. God chose and sent Jesus as the promised Savior and Deliverer. Although many Jews today disagree, we do not argue with them.

As a Christian, a follower of Jesus Christ, this is our statement of faith and a declaration of our allegiance, commitment, and submission to Jesus Christ. This is how we will bring Jesus Christ back to the forefront of our personal lives, the Church, and out into the world: by breathing, eating, and sleeping Jesus. Jesus Christ is not just some "fly-by-night" guy whom we can spin any way we want, use to our benefit, or manipulate. No, He is God Himself, who holds ultimate authority and is the source of salvation for the world. When people believe His story, as it's written, and emulate His words and actions, and then share this with the world, Jesus will once again be in charge of their lives.

There is something special and unique about Jesus' name as it relates to God. It's why you may hear people mention God or having a belief in Him, or professing a relationship with God, but they leave out Jesus' name; they believe in God but not Jesus. It's not possible. As I stressed throughout this book, Jesus is the only way to come into a relationship with God. God named Jesus and gave Him the authority and keys to His kingdom--to run it. All we just read about what Jesus suffered and endured qualified Him to obtain this rank.

Praying to God often (in Jesus' name), reading the Bible to understand Jesus' lessons, and using them every day will help us to keep Jesus up front. Acts of service to others can show His love and compassion in tangible ways. These practices help solidify our faith in Jesus, ensuring He remains at the center of our lives and the world.

Sharing in Jesus Christ's suffering is a part of the Christian walk. It's not about accumulating a lot of money, getting a big dream house or fancy car, landing an ideal, promising job, affording and wearing the latest fashions, building mega churches and attracting thousands, receiving prominent church titles, drawing thousands to our concerts, performing on a large stage, or amassing hundreds of social media followers—as is promoted today. If you don't believe me or think I'm being negative, pessimistic, or extreme, read Matthew 24:9, Luke 6:22, and John 15:18-21. Jesus repeatedly told His disciples they would suffer and be hated for bearing His name. Some of Jesus' other disciples (like some of us now) turned back because these teachings were too difficult. "This is a bit much," we think. (See John 6:48-69.) Regarding the great apostle Paul, Acts 9:16 says about him, *"For I will show him how much he must suffer for the sake of my name."* However, this is not something we should shrink from. Jesus promised that in every trial, He will walk with us, offering hope, grace, and comfort, because He endured every type of trial and suffering (John 16:33), which should encourage us. Look again at the abuse He suffered. As you share in His suffering, know that He also shares in your burdens, helping you to carry them. Trust that through every pain and difficulty, this is how God molds us into His likeness and draws us closer to Him.

Now, forgive my candor here, but is this what is going on in Christendom today? Are we being hated, despised, or persecuted? We do almost anything to avoid being disliked, more so hated. Around the world, there are some Christians who are being persecuted for disagreeing with their country's government, religion, communism, Islamic extremism, or culture.

Here in America, however, we appear to be in good standing and are receiving acceptance and applause. They're not hating on us, but, in fact, seem to love networking with Christians. Why? We complain to them, seek their advice, put other believers "on blast," and provide media interviews about their or a church's faults and failures. Instead of remaining unified and dealing with our frailties among the body of believers who think like us and restoring our brothers and sisters in Christ (as the Bible tells us to), we're running to tell the world about it and discussing our problems with them, seeking their advice. There's a reason Christ warned the Church to remain unified.

We have formed alliances with the world, making business/financial/ contractual deals, scheduling speaking engagements on various outlets to be seen and heard, and performing with secular artists who do not even believe in Jesus Christ. We cut deals with the world, taking their money, and on and on it goes. We've incorporated their worldview. OMG!

Why are we like this? Because we are earthly-minded and worldly (and I'm not referring to things we've *categorized* as sinful behaviors—like smoking, drinking, sexual immorality, homosexuality, cheating, lying, stealing, etc.). We're worldly when we think as the world does. When we do not take Jesus' name or mission to heart, we're worldly. When we don't take His words to heart about growth and transformation via suffering and pain, we're worldly. We've opted for the world's appealing, easier, profitable "glorified position" to Jesus' teachings about what pain produces. We don't even realize how much we're dug in. Now, some of you may think, "Well, this was Jesus' message for the disciples back then." No. Remember, we looked at John 17, where Jesus prayed for His disciples and included all future believers when He prayed in verse 20: *"My prayer is not for them alone." I pray also for those who will believe in me through their message.* Did you believe in Jesus' message after that writing? Then that's for us.

In addition, the apostle Paul also experienced suffering (a thorn in his flesh). He so wonderfully explains this concept in Philippians 3:7-11 (NIV). He writes,

> *Further, my brothers and sisters, rejoice in the Lord! It is no trouble for me to write the same things to you again, and it is a safeguard for you. Watch out for those dogs, those evildoers, those mutilators of the flesh. For it is we who are the circumcision,*

we who serve God by his Spirit, who boast in Christ Jesus, and who put no confidence in the flesh—though I myself have reasons for such confidence. If someone else thinks they have reasons to put confidence in the flesh, I have more: circumcised on the eighth day, of the people of Israel, of the tribe of Benjamin, a Hebrew of Hebrews; in regard to the law, a Pharisee; as for zeal, persecuting the church; as for righteousness based on the law, faultless. But whatever were gains to me I now consider loss for the sake of Christ. What is more, I consider everything a loss because of the surpassing worth of knowing Christ Jesus my Lord, for whose sake I have lost all things. I consider them garbage, that I may gain Christ and be found in him, not having a righteousness of my own that comes from the law, but that which is through faith in Christ—the righteousness that comes from God on the basis of faith. I want to know Christ—yes, to know the power of his resurrection and participation in his sufferings, becoming like him in his death, and so, somehow, attaining to the resurrection from the dead.

Paul's words resonate with me. I love what He's saying here. I get it! (Many "Christians" don't.) He first warns us to "Watch out!"—not against literal murderers, but against those who insist on religious performance, good acts, or deeds to earn Christ's acceptance. Paul says that if righteousness came from such work, he could confidently boast. e was educated, kept the law, and was faultless; he was zealous in persecuting Christians. He came to realize, however, as I have, that these accomplishments, skills, and zeal for wrongdoing were worthless compared to knowing Jesus. In fact, He considers everything a loss compared to what He's gained in knowing Christ; it's rubbish.

Do we think this way? Are we okay about losing to know Jesus, to keep Him first—if it comes to that? That is the essence of the Christian walk, not the external "blessings" and material things others are now emphasizing. The blessings we looked at from God earlier in Ephesians were all spiritual blessings, not material. Don't misunderstand me. God might give some of you wealth, a lot of material possessions, and a lucrative lifestyle, but that's not the most important part of His plan for saving you. You may still suffer for Jesus Christ with all this luxury.

In the Christian life, we gain by losing; we know Christ by denying and debasing ourselves; we give to get—a foreign concept that is *not* promoted in our culture, our society. This idea of fellowship in Jesus' sufferings means turning your losses, pain, and trials over to the Lord and recalling Jesus Christ's sufferings and taking on His perspective.

I realize that there are some painful situations, some traumas, some types of suffering that take time to get over; you may not initially have this perspective, but, as a Christian, you ultimately get there.

A journey with Jesus Christ and coming to know Him intimately involves three aspects, Paul seems to allude to in Philippians 3. We *want* to know Jesus in all three aspects:

- **in the power of His resurrection (the highs)**
- **fellowship with Him in what He suffered (the painful lows)**
- **becoming like Him in His death (the process of humility where we ultimately take on His perspective)**

That's deep! And that's the difference, the key. Jesus Christ is at the forefront when we can adopt Paul's sentiments here. All the things we love, have gained, desire, are exceptional at, or do well, are nothing compared to finding and knowing Jesus Christ. Jesus is at the forefront of your life when you can funnel all your pain, your suffering, your loss through His lens, what He's been through. When you view your pain and suffering as God does and remain as Jesus did in it, Jesus Christ is at the forefront. You don't act like the world by retaliating or getting even; complaining and blaming others; seething in frustration, anger, and bitterness—even against yourself; or cheating to get ahead.

As Philippians 3:10 teaches us, as a follower of Jesus Christ, we are experiencing a change of heart. We are sacrificing, denying ourselves, and practicing humility. These are the ways of Jesus Christ. Boy, do we have this wrong. OMG! I believe the Bible Project says in one of their videos how God's kingdom is an upside-down one; isn't that the truth? We need to bring Jesus Christ back to the forefront. OMG!

All of this happens when we do what the opening verse suggests: *Fix our eyes on Jesus.* Life won't spin out of control when we keep Jesus on our minds, place Him first, and keep Him at the center of our hearts.

God has placed some of us in godly families. We met and networked with godly Christians. We belong to good churches where the ministers, priests, or leaders are exceptional, and the members are supportive. We have close friendships with other Christians who are upholding and serving Christ. This is wonderful! But still our eyes remain fixed on Jesus. As great as these experiences may be. As much as we learn and grow from them, our eyes must always remain fixed on Jesus, remembering what He said and did, and modeling our lives after Him. He is the preeminent One, taking first place over everyone and everything.

Jesus Christ and Me Today

I'm 63 years old now.

Two of the best things Jesus Christ has done in my life are to keep me balanced--aware of *what I'm not* in comparison to Jesus Christ, while understanding what I am in Him--and weaning me from being so people-dependent. I began this book, saying, "No one noticed." Now, I've grown in Christ not to care so much about who notices. God notices, and that is all that matters to me.

It's nice when God takes precedence over everyone and everything in your life. When we hear Him say to us, "I've done a work in you in that area," it relaxes us, takes off that pressure. You see, I've discerned that sometimes, in this journey with Jesus, you recognize how some people are projecting onto you what is true about themselves. (Projection, a word I heard Mom repeat before her death). People are so hard on you to live up to their standards or run your life because they really believe theirs is the right way you should go. That's why we must understand that a relationship with Jesus Christ is unique to everyone.

Part of His weaning process for me from people dependency has happened by allowing me to be in this suffering posture for about 15 years now. I'm getting to know Christ intimately, and I like Him better than people. LOL.

At about age 36, I left academia and tried going out on my own in business. I launched a business that offered remote virtual assistant services to various clients. I thought since I was so exceptional behind the desk, I could do this better for others on my own. I wasn't sure at first and scared. God supported me, however, by giving me all the start-up equipment—a computer, printer, fax machine, copier, etc. (It's a long story how He gave it to me, but if you send me an email or call and ask, I'll tell you.) I was eager, earnest, and again, thought only about being a successful business owner. I conducted research, studied the industry, and conducted market analysis. Things were going well for a while, and my boyfriend at that time helped. I even had my son, twelve then, photocopying and assembling papers. I worked around the clock and harder than I had. After a while, business slowed substantially, and I had to take on some temporary work. I ran the business for about ten years until it eventually folded. I learned that it's one thing to excel behind your desk, but it's another thing to work with competitors. You need money and sound equipment to compete in business.

At about age 46-47, while doing temporary work, I started having health problems that made me go to the Philadelphia hospital emergency rooms often. They all said the same thing: I was having a mental health crisis. I kept telling them, "There's something wrong with my body." They insisted I needed a psychiatric evaluation, maybe because they had records of schizophrenia in my family. It consumed my oldest brother, who ended up homeless because of it, all because he could never accept that he had it. I remember going to my cousin's law firm to borrow money; he, too, tried to help me and take me to the hospital for a mental evaluation, but I was afraid and didn't go with him.

I finally consented to a mental evaluation and spent two weeks in the hospital psychiatric ward. While there, I met a doctor who was a psychiatrist and neurologist. She asked me to repeat my symptoms. I did; she ordered tests and later told me I had multiple sclerosis (MS). I was 48 years old.

I took it in stride, but my mind immediately flashed to the Jerry Lewis muscular dystrophy campaigns he used to do on television every year. The doctor explained that this was a different disease. I left the hospital and returned home in relatively good spirits.

"MS isn't so bad after all," I thought, until the symptoms started rapidly worsening. It began to alter every part of my body function, my hands the most, and my legs, eyes, rib cage, bladder, and on and on. I was a typist and asked the Lord, "Why my hands?" Like Paul was faultless in the law, the documents I transcribed were flawless. When I delivered them, you did not see those blue or red underlines that you see in Microsoft Word. By the way, it was my father who once told me, "You have healing hands."

I went into a deep depression and stayed in my room most days. My balance was off, I made frequent trips to the bathroom, my feet and hands were constantly numb, and spasticity was all over my body. I could not move as fast anymore. Once, I woke up from a nap and could not see the center of people's faces; they immediately admitted me into the hospital. Ugh! This was my new life with MS—hospitals, steroids, medicines, frequent bathroom breaks, brain fog, a much slower pace, and no more administrative work. The last two temp jobs I attempted let me go. I no longer had the speed, accuracy, or multitasking ability. I told you how much I loved my line of work. This hurt and burst my bubble. OMG!

Sharing in Christ's sufferings. This is it (when our mindset eventually becomes like Christ in everything we go through). I did not know I would lose most of what I loved and had confidence in, but God did. My speed was gone, my coordination and balance off, my hands always tight and numb, and my career forever gone. I lived in denial for a while until the Lord spoke very clearly to me, as I was trying to move like I once did, "You're sick, Ellie." (Now, many in the faith word movement would consider this a negative confession and may say, that wasn't the Lord talking to me.) OMG! Anyway, my son also helped by reminding me to slow down or use the mobility aids. I had to accept the truth and learn to live life anew with MS.

I stayed with Jesus, and for 15 years, He has helped me to readjust my life with this disease. We frequently equate truth solely with knowing the Bible scriptures. But God operates in truth in our everyday lives by making the truth of Scripture come alive in our real-life circumstances. He reveals the truth about what's happening on Earth. Multiple sclerosis or its symptoms are not written in the Bible. God knows and sees all and has guided me through the realities that happen in my day-to-day life. We trust in and rely on God's omniscience and providence.

I sometimes laugh when people comment on our family photos, saying what a beautiful family we are, and don't get me wrong, we are blessed. However, Catherine and Richard Parks' family have a cross to bear. What people do not know about us is the various painful situations we've all had to endure. The crosses we had to bear, the sharing in Christ's suffering we had to endure. Each of my siblings could tell you their own testimonies of the pain and suffering they had to walk through; it's what keeps each one of us connected to the Lord. Pain and suffering that caused us to grow, to remain humble, to change us, to love Him more, and to stay with and keep Him front and center in our lives.

I completed this manuscript and formatted it for Amazon with numb, shaking hands. with tremors. I discovered Romans 8:26 Is true, how*, [the Holy Spirit] "helps us in our weakness;"* and 2 Corinthians 12:9, which says, *"[His] power is made perfect in weakness,"* and Isaiah 40:29, *"He gives strength to the weary and increases the power of* *the weak."* Boy, has MS weakened me. No "be strong," power words in those verses, are there? It truly is an upside-down kingdom! LOL.

Huh? Some of you are thinking. How can pain and suffering make someone draw closer? We're taught the opposite—avoid and get away from anyone causing you pain and sadness. While this may be true, not trouble or pain the Lord wills for being connected with Jesus. Has the Lord ever told you to stay in a place or deal with a person that troubles you? Jesus did; the Pharisees and Sadducees constantly battled Jesus. Has the Lord ever told you not to follow the group (or crowd) that is against a particular person? You talk to or deal with them?

See, there is glory amid pain, and after it (Isaiah 40:5; Luke 24:56). Suffering always precedes glory, just as Jesus received glory. He was exalted to a higher place with God. For Christians, we grow from pain, we develop divine attributes, become better, and are perfected by painful situations. This is the upside-down kingdom the Bible Project talks about. It does not teach or promote what our culture does. OMG!

In one of His lessons with His disciples, they had left the Jerusalem temple and were telling Jesus how impressed they were by it. Jesus tells them the truth by saying in Matthew 24:1-2, *Jesus left the temple and was walking away when his disciples came up to him to call his attention to its buildings. "Do you see all these things?" he asks. "Truly I tell you, not one stone here will be left on another; every one will be thrown down.*

See, the ideology of the world is to rely on world systems, people, and things. Jesus is coming again to establish His kingdom on earth, and everything in this world, as it is, will cease. Not only will buildings cease, but so will the people we love, rely on, and learn from. This, too, has weaned me from people dependency and idolization. You see, I lost my grandfather, Poppie in 1978, my eldest brother, Rick in 2005, my dad in 2008, my eldest sis, Chris, in 2013, my mom in 2014, and most recently, my third eldest sister, Dr. Carolyn Parks, in 2024.

We just had a big party for Carol to celebrate her retirement and 70th birthday. Carol was my sister, who was often away from us while in graduate school and later as a university professor. In all her pursuits, however, she remembered everyone's birthday and always got back to you if you called. She was not responding to our texts or phone calls, and both my son and I noticed she had not posted on Facebook for his youngest daughter's birthday. My sister advised me to get to her place right away. I did, and there she was, deceased, on her bed. She wasn't seriously ill, except that she told my sister and me how she had tested positive for COVID a third time and was having occasional episodes of malaise. We encouraged her to see a doctor, but death never entered our minds.

We were planning to do life with her after retirement. But it seemed, with no warning, she just vanished. James 4:14 came to my mind, which says, *"Our life is like a vapor."* I've read or heard that verse quoted for years, but it came alive, and I understood it through my sister's death. She seemed to have just evaporated into the air. She was to be an editor for this book. I still ache and cry sometimes, but the Lord knows everything. Remember, Jesus wept at Lazarus' death? Jesus walked through and felt the pains of life, too. He has not answered my why questions about my sister, but I trust His judgment.

You see, it is in these sufferings that we learn, we grow, we adopt Jesus' attitude and perspective, and we should learn to wear this world loosely; God's kingdom is forever, not anything in this world. That's what Jesus instilled in His disciples.

Donnie McClurkin and Marvin Winans recorded a song entitled "Who Would've Thought." I like the music and lyrics because it's how I look at my life. You can find it on YouTube or Spotify. Some of the lyrics say:

> *"Heard folk talk about the things you've done, and I would just laugh at what they say...*
> *Who would've thought in time that I would be the one?*
> *Who would've thought that I'd get to know you this way?*
> *You came and took my life and made it brand new....*
> *You took me in as one of your own...*
> *Now, when I feel my life is falling apart, I could just bend my knees and pray...*
> *I got to know you for myself...*
> *So glad I know you!"* (McClurkin D. and Winans M.)

Who would've thought a woman like me–the youngest, with body image issues, personality disorders, a low self-esteem; is mostly unfeminine, too talkative at times, doubtful, prideful and arrogant, energetic, quick-moving, disrespectful, self-centered, ambitious, a worrier, anxious, depressed, oppressed, manipulative, tardy, wasteful, a procrastinator, comparer, with some not so good habits, and undisciplined—would write a book about Jesus Christ? (Hallelujah! Would you get up, rejoice, and dance with me—

and Jesus, of course?) LOL.

This is where my life is at now with Jesus--getting to know Him more and amazed at how far He's brought me. I have joy! I'm content! And I can't understand how the Lord pulled off something like this in a misdirected girl like me. OMG!

Additionally, during the research, writing, editing, and publication of this book, I identified areas in my life where I can bring Christ back to the forefront. How about you? How will you bring Jesus Christ back to His rightful place in your life? That's between Him and you.

Two Final Stories

Forgiveness Sets Me Free

Before Mom passed from this life, she released me from the debt I owed her because of my horrible mouth. She was scheduled for a vascular procedure at the hospital. She called me the day before that test and said to me, "Ellie, I want you to know that everything with you and me is all right. I forgive you for everything you said to me. You had a mouth, and so did I." Not only did Mom forgive me, but she also let me know she, too, had the same problem with her mouth that I did. Wow!

I didn't know what to say. I apologized again and told her how sorry I was for disrespecting her. We laughed and rejoiced as we hung up. Relieved that I had had this conversation with Mom, I went to bed and drifted off to sleep. Upon awakening the next morning, I learned Mom had had a stroke during the night. The stroke took her voice, and Mom could not talk to us for six months before she eventually died. OMG! I just broke down and cried. I thought, suppose Mom had never called me or put off or procrastinated as I did with the professor at my job. Suppose she had a prideful attitude, like I was just her youngest daughter who didn't know any better, so don't bother. Some recalled my evil ways and have an air when I tell that story, as if I didn't deserve that from Mom. But I heard from the horse's mouth. I know Mom's forgiveness was God's forgiveness to set me free and keep me living. I needed that because my actions troubled me.

Don't Despise the Small Deeds of Your Past

My final story involves the first child I ever tutored, Evander (Van). He was about ten years old when I began tutoring him, and I was 20. (I still tutor middle school children in reading and ELA today to supplement my disability income.) I helped Van complete his homework and made sure he understood it. He was a smart kid and had the best laugh ever. I had interactions with him before this; his mom, aunt, and I were friends; in fact, I hung out at their house often.

He's about 52 years old now, and he called me the other day. I thought something had happened. He assured me that everything was okay. He had a dream about my niece and me, where he was at our home, just hanging out with us. He called just to say hello. No doubt, I was surprised but happy he did. We chatted about those tutoring days, our former neighbors, and laughed about the different nicknames he and others had. It was great!

Then Van became serious. He began talking about the things he's been going through. I listened. He felt as if things were going on in his life for a reason. He said, "like a guy I met on the job that I've been talking with. He's a Christian and has been talking to me about the Lord." That was my cue.

I asked Van, "Do you feel like God is calling you?" He immediately said, "Yes!" I assured Van that it was God's love drawing him. I shared a bit of my testimony about my relationship with Jesus, but not much. I told him how different I am from how I used to be. You see, Van witnessed the not-so-good parts of me. We did a lot of wrong things in front of Van; he saw and heard it all. I suggested he share some of his struggles with the guy at his job, and I left him with the idea that if the Lord changed me, He could change him, too. I hung up after our conversation, overjoyed and ecstatic!

Now, was his dream, his phone call, the guy at work — all a coincidence? I don't think so. That was God, and that's how He works sometimes. He wants Van, and if the guy at work doesn't get him first, I'm reeling him for Jesus! That's what's up!

Would you help me lift Jesus higher, as Gospel recording artist, Fred Hammond, exhorts us to? Listen at https://youtu.be/3xLNTxaF2ps?si=tZrBz1bhlsCfP_Y0.

Hopefully, you're able to visualize what I do most days by the music links I share. My home is God's sanctuary. I don't have to wait for Sunday services. My odd-shaped body is a vessel of praise, anytime, anywhere — on public transportation, in an Uber, on CCT to the doctor, at home, every day. With my walker so I won't fall, I dance to the Lord with my big feet, long hands, and boisterous personality! (Thanks for introducing the headsets, younger Gen!) LOL.

Maybe this is one way some of you can begin to bring Christ back to the forefront--simply begin to praise Him, regardless of your predicament!

Receive Salvation in Jesus Christ

Maybe you've never heard about Jesus Christ. This is your first time hearing His story. Well, the apostle Paul tells us good news about Jesus Christ in 1 Corinthians 15:3-5 (NIV) from the Bible. It says, *For what I received I passed on to you as of first importance that Christ died for our sins according to the Scriptures, that he was buried, that he was raised on the third day according to the Scriptures, and that he appeared to Cephas, and then to the Twelve.*

Jesus really did this for you, my friend. John 3:16-17 (NIV) tells us why Jesus did this. It says, *For God so loved the world that he gave his one and only Son, that whoever believes in him shall not perish but have eternal life. For God did not send his Son into the world to condemn the world, but to save the world through him.*

Out of a heart of love, God sent His Son, Jesus, to us, for us! Everyone aspires to be loved. We search high and low sometimes seeking it, don't we? I'm introducing to you today the most excellent lover of all time. I know. I invited Jesus into my heart as a teenager, and He hasn't stopped showing me His love since.

God wants you to believe and receive this truth about his Son, Jesus Christ. Believe He came from God, died for your sins, was buried, and rose again to give you eternal life with God.

Wherever you are right now, tell God you believe the message about Jesus Christ, and ask Him to come into your heart and make you the person He created you to be. That's it. He will come in, and you'll know it!

If you said this prayer, let us know by emailing me at elliedp1@outlook.com

If You've Lost Your Way

If you have lost your way and know you need to bring Christ back into your life. Read how Jesus restored His disciple, Peter. Peter was the audacious disciple who, when the heat hit Jesus' life, cursed, and swore that he wasn't with Him and had never known Jesus.

In John 21, Jesus restores Peter, who betrayed Him, by reinstating him as a leader and commissioning him to care for his flock. The scene takes place on the shore of the Sea of Galilee, where Jesus has prepared a meal and invites the disciples to join him. After breakfast, Jesus engages Peter in a conversation, asking him three times, "Simon, son of John, do you love me?" Each time Peter affirms his love for Jesus. Jesus instructs him to "feed my lambs" and "take care of my sheep. This act signifies Peter's forgiveness and reinstatement into ministry. Each time, Peter responds affirmatively, and Jesus gives him a specific task related to his flock: "Feed my lambs," "Tend my sheep," and "Feed my sheep." These instructions mirror Peter's earlier denial, and the threefold questioning is seen as a way to address his three denials. The repetition also underscores Peter's love and care for Jesus' followers.

Through this restoration, Jesus not only forgives Peter but also reinstates him as a leader in the early church. This act of restoration is a powerful example of God's grace and forgiveness, showing that even after failure, there is an opportunity for restoration and service.

Like I needed restoration from my mother, in what way do you need restoration through Jesus Christ? Do you truly love Jesus but got tripped up some kind of way? Tell the Lord about it, where you went wrong, and receive His mercy, grace, and forgiveness.

Be restored, my friends, and "Go!"

Stay with Jesus

End with Jesus

About the Author

Eleanor ("Ellie") Parks is a born-again follower of Jesus Christ. A lifelong passion for writing, this is her first published work. Raised in Philadelphia, she is the youngest of seven children. She first learned about Jesus at home but found Him in her teenage years. Her blog, *Inspiration by Ellie*, discusses the Bible, combining it with everyday life situations to show God's activity in the world.

She holds a degree in biblical studies from Colorado Christian University. She is a single mother to her son, Bryant, and his wife, Kelly, and has three beautiful granddaughters, whom she refers to as her "A" girls: Amiyah, Azariah, and Ayla. She enjoys discussing the Bible, meeting new people, the computer, asking questions, and playing Pac-Man.

Bibliography

Auten, Brian. "Apologetics 315." 11 October 2013. *Apologetics Toolkit: Tips for Lifelong Learning #01.* 1 february 2022. <https://apologetics315.com/2013/10/apologetics-toolkit-tips-for-lifelong-learning-01/>.

Barth, K, T.F. Torrance, G. W. Bromiley. "The Election of God, The Command of God." *Church Dogmatics The Doctrine of God* 2004.

Battle, John A. "Charles Hodge, Inspiration, Textual Criticism, and The Princeton Doctrine of Scripture." *The Christian Observer: The Presbyterian & Reformed Journal for 200 years - 1813-2013* 198 (2009): 17:27. https://christianobserver.org/charles-hodge-inspiration-textual-criticism-and-the-princeton-doctrine-of-scripture/#:~:text=Nature%20of%20Inspiration,used%20men%20as%20they%20were.

BibleHub. "Mockery." *Topical Encyclopedia*. n.d. https://biblehub.com/topical/m/mockery.htm.

Carter, Craig A. *Interpreting Scripture with the Great Tradition: Recovering the Genius of Premodern Exegesis*. ProQuest Ebook Central. Baker Academic, 2018. <https://ebookcentral.proquest.com/lib/cochristuniv-ebooks/reader.action?docID=5371920&ppg=1&c=UERG>.

"Christianity 201." 13 October 2019. *Christianity 201.* <https://christianity201.wordpress.com/2019/10/13/jehovah-names-of-god/>.

Christianity.com. "Christianity.com." 29 January 2024. *What Is Prophecy? Bible Meaning and Examples of Prophesy.* 2024. <https://www.christianity.com/wiki/christian-terms/what-is-prophecy-meaning-of-prophesy.html>.

Clowney, Edmund. *The Unfolding Mystery: Discovering Christ in the Old Testament*. 2013.

Easton's Bible Dictionary. "Reconciling." *Easton's Bible Dictionary*. n.d. https://www.biblegateway.com/passage/?search=2%20Corinthians%205%3A19-21%20&version=NET.

Elwell, Walter A. ""Entry for 'Jesus Christ'"." *Evangelical Dictionary of Theology*. Ed. Walter A. Elwell. Baker's Books A Division of Baker's Evangelical Dictionary of Biblical Theology. Grand Rapids: Baker's Books, 1997. <https://www.biblestudytools.com/dictionaries/bakers-evangelical-dictionary/jesus-christ.html>.

Erickson, Milllard J. *Introducing Christian Doctrine (2nd ed.)*. Grand Rapids: Baker, 2001.

Google A.I. n.d.

Google AI Overview. June 3 2025.

GotQuestions Ministries. "Why are there so many Christian denominations?" n.d. *Got Questions.* https://www.gotquestions.org/denominations-Christian.html. 23 December 2025.

GotQuestions.org. "What is the history of crucifixion?" 28 August 2024. *Got Questions Ministries* . https://www.gotquestions.org/crucifixion.html. August 2025.

Kaiser, Walter. "The Bible." 2001: 209, 211.

Kant, Immanuel. "What is Enlightment?" 30 September 1784.

Kim, Jay Y. ""Faith Gateway. The True Center (from Session 1 of Colossians)." n.d. *Jesus is the divine center of all things.*

Matthew Henry's Commentary on the Bible. *Entry for John 19:30, He bowed his head and gave up the ghost*. Biblical Studies Press, L.L.C. , 1996-2017. Retrieved from https://www.biblegateway.com/passage/?search=John%2019%3A29%2D31&version=NIV.

McClurkin D. and Winans M. "Who Would've Thought." By Donnie McClurkin. Zomba Recording LLC, 2000.

https://www.youtube.com/watch?v=fnKzc6yHCOU&list=RDfnKzc6yHCOU &start_radio=1.

McGrath, Alister E. *Christian Theology*. West Sussex, United Kingdom: Wiley-Blackwell Publishing, 2011.

Mears, Henrietta. *What the Bible is All About*. Ventura: Regal Books a ministry of Gospel Light, 1998.

Merkle, Benjamin L. "The Teachings of Jesus." 2025. *TGC US Edition.* 2024. <https://www.thegospelcoalition.org/essay/the-teachings-of-jesus-2/>.

Neel Burton, M.A, M.D. "The Psychology of Humiliation. What is humiliation and can it ever be justified?" 28 February 2025. https://www.psychologytoday.com/us/blog/hide-and-seek/201408/the-psychology-of-humiliation.

NIH, National Library of Medicine, National Center for Biotechnology Information. "Abuse." n.d. https://www.ncbi.nlm.nih.gov/pmc/articles/PMC8060108/).

Snodgrass, Klynne. *The NIV Application Commentary: Ephesians*. Grand Rapids: Zondervan, 1996.

Sproul, R.C. "Divine Illumination." 14 June 2014. *Ligonier Ministries.* 30 May 2025. <https://learn.ligonier.org/devotionals/divine-illumination>.

—. "Preaching and Teaching." 13 June 2024. *Ligonier Ministries.* <https://learn.ligonier.org/articles/preaching-and-teaching>.

—. "In the Heavenlies ." 2025. *Ray Stedman: Authentic Christianity.* 15 January 2025. <https://www.raystedman.org/daily-devotions/ephesians/in-the-heavenlies>.

—. "The Necessity of the Cross." 14 January 2025. *Ray Stedman: Authentic Christianity.* https://www.raystedman.org/daily-devotions/mark/the-necessity-of-the-cross. August 2025.

—. *The Need for Death*. 20 December 2025. https://www.raystedman.org/daily-devotions/hebrews/the-need-for-death.

Stetzer, E. "SmallGroups.com Build a Thriving Communty." 2025. *Christianity Today International. Used by permission.* 2024. <https://www.smallgroups.com/articles/2015/epidemic-of-bible-illiteracy-in-our-churches.html#:~:text=Small%20groups%20must%20provide%20a,issues%20and%20apply%20God's%20Word.>.

Stokes, Pastor Virgil. "We're Glad You're Here." 2 August 2025. *Pastor Virgil.com.* Pastor Virgil Stokes. 2 August 2025. <https://pastorvirgil.com/2025/08/02/were-glad-youre-here/>.

Swindoll, Pastor Chuck. "Insight for Living Canada." December 2022. *Insight for Living Canada. The Bible Teaching Ministry of Charles L. Swindoll.* 20 May 2025. <https://www.insightforliving.ca/read/articles/god-all-problems-eventually-fade>.

The ESV Global Study Bible. *JOHN—NOTE ON 19:30 It is finished*. Crossway, 2012. https://www.biblegateway.com/passage/?search=John%2019%3A29%2D31&version=NIV.

The NIV Jesus Bible. *It is Finished*. Zondervan, 2016. https://www.biblegateway.com/.

Wikipedia, The Free Encyclopedia. *Holy Spirit in Christianity*. n.d. https://en.wikipedia.org/wiki/Holy_Spirit_in_Christianity. January 2025.

www.ingramcontent.com/pod-product-compliance
Lightning Source LLC
LaVergne TN
LVHW061223100826
845148LV00004B/835

* 9 7 9 8 2 1 8 8 7 3 4 3 1 *